One-day women's event, hosted by **BRF** and **Woman Alive**

God's resource for life's challenges:
How the Psalms can help us pray through all life experiences

Saturday 15 June 2019

Guildford Baptist Church

Millmead, Guildford GU2 4BE

Speakers • Worship • Fellowship • Talks • Bookstall

Take a look at all BRF events at

brfonline.org.uk/events-and-quiet-days

The Bible Reading Fellowship
15 The Chambers, Vineyard
Abingdon OX14 3FE
brf.org.uk

The Bible Reading Fellowship (BRF) is a Registered Charity (233280)

This edition © The Bible Reading Fellowship 2019
Cover image © Thinkstock

Distributed in Australia by:
MediaCom Education Inc, PO Box 610, Unley, SA 5061
Tel: 1 800 811 311 | admin@mediacom.org.au

Distributed in New Zealand by:
Scripture Union Wholesale, PO Box 760, Wellington
Tel: 04 385 0421 | suwholesale@clear.net.nz

Acknowledgements

Scripture quotations marked NIV taken from The Holy Bible, New International Version (Anglicised edition) copyright © 1979, 1984, 2011 by Biblica. Used by permission of Hodder & Stoughton Publishers, a Hachette UK company. All rights reserved. 'NIV' is a registered trademark of Biblica. UK trademark number 1448790. • Scripture quotations marked MSG are taken from *The Message*, copyright © 1993, 1994, 1995, 1996, 2000, 2001, 2002 by Eugene H. Peterson. Used by permission of NavPress. All rights reserved. Represented by Tyndale House Publishers, Inc. • Scripture quotations marked NLT taken from the Holy Bible, New Living Translation, copyright © 1996, 2004, 2007, 2013. Used by permission of Tyndale House Publishers, Inc., Carol Stream, Illinois 60188. All rights reserved. • Scripture taken from The Source: With Extensive Notes on Greek Word Meaning. Copyright © 2004 by Ann Nyland. Used by permission of Smith and Stirling Publishers. All rights reserved. • Scripture quotations marked GNT from the Good News Bible published by The Bible Societies/HarperCollins Publishers Ltd, UK © American Bible Society 1966, 1971, 1976, 1992, used with permission. • Scripture quotations marked CEV from the Contemporary English Version. New Testament © American Bible Society 1991, 1992, 1995. Old Testament © American Bible Society 1995. Anglicisations © British & Foreign Bible Society 1996. Used by permission. • Scripture quotations marked NRSV from The New Revised Standard Version of the Bible, Anglicised edition, copyright © 1989, 1995 by the Division of Christian Education of the National Council of the Churches of Christ in the United States of America. Used by permission. All rights reserved. • Scripture quotations marked TLB from The Living Bible copyright © 1971 by Tyndale House Foundation. Used by permission of Tyndale House Publishers Inc., Carol Stream, Illinois 60188. All rights reserved. • Scripture quotations marked TPT from The Passion Translation®. Copyright © 2017 by BroadStreet Publishing® Group, LLC. Used by permission. All rights reserved. thePassionTranslation.com • Scripture quotations marked NASB taken from the New American Standard Bible®, Copyright © 1960, 1962, 1963, 1968, 1971, 1972, 1973, 1975, 1977, 1995 by The Lockman Foundation. Used by permission. (Lockman.org) • Scripture quotations marked ESV taken from the Holy Bible, English Standard Version, published by HarperCollins Publishers, © 2001 Crossway Bibles, a division of Good News Publishers. Used by permission. All rights reserved.

Every effort has been made to trace and contact copyright owners for material used in this resource. We apologise for any inadvertent omissions or errors, and would ask those concerned to contact us so that full acknowledgement can be made in the future.

A catalogue record for this book is available from the British Library

Printed by Gutenberg Press, Tarxien, Malta

Day by Day
with
God

Edited by **Ali Herbert** and **Jill Rattle**   **May–August 2019**

Writers in this issue

Chris Leonard lives in Surrey with her husband. They have three young grandchildren and Chris remains busy leading creative writing courses and holidays. She has had a total of 21 books published.

Christine Platt lives in New Zealand and enjoys the freedom and opportunities that retirement brings. As well as encouraging mission in her church, she also teaches English to Chinese people locally and to young people in East Timor.

Sheila Jacobs is a writer, an editor and an award-winning author. She lives in rural north Essex, attends an Elim church, where she serves as a deacon, and is a day chaplain at a retreat centre.

Claire Musters is a speaker, a writer and an editor with a passion to see people reach their full potential in God. She has written many books, including *Taking Off the Mask* (Authentic Media, 2017). Find out more at **clairemusters.com**.

Michele D. Morrison and her husband Don are working on their bucket list, babysitting their grandchildren and aiding her nonagenarian mother. Michele also edits the church magazine, writing and blogging at **tearsamidthealiencorn.blogspot.com**.

Sara Batts was previously a specialist librarian and is now a priest in the Diocese of Chelmsford. She lives with a dog and hosts a cat.

Fiona Barnard is a TEFL/ESOL teacher and staff member of Friends International. She works with international students, encouraging local Christians to reach out in friendship and evangelism to make disciples. She is an honorary chaplain at the University of St Andrews, Scotland.

Lyndall Bywater is married to Phil and lives in Canterbury. She is a freelance writer and speaker, and her favourite subject is prayer.

Caroline Fletcher is a freelance writer. She has an MPhil in biblical studies and trained as an RE teacher. She is married to a vicar and is involved in all-age services and youth work at her church in Sheffield.

Jennifer Rees Larcombe runs Beauty from Ashes, an organisation that supports people adjusting to bereavement and trauma. She lives in the Kentish countryside with her little dog Noah, and loves gardening and entertaining her 15 grandchildren.

Jill Rattle and Ali Herbert write...

Jill: While my husband and I were preparing to move to Birmingham, we lodged for 15 months in half a house that was joined to the other half by a locked door connecting the lounges. We could hear people talking and laughing on the other side, but their voices were too muffled to hear what was being said. Often, when the laughter rose, we wished we could hear clearly and join in! But that was only possible on the occasions when the door was opened.

It is through reading God's word that we hear his voice but, for most of us, his voice is sometimes a bit muffled and we wish we could hear him better and join in with him more. Our contributors, who prayerfully write these notes, want to help 'open the door' so that we will encounter him more fully and share with him the laughter and the laments of our daily life. With each reading, we also need to open the door of our hearts to him and be ready to receive what he has for us that day.

Ali: As we head into the (hopefully sunny) summer months, it might seem strange to begin with Chris Leonard looking at the topic of lament in the Psalms. However, the psalms are nothing if not real. While they hit the heights of praise, worship and joy, they are never afraid to tackle the darker side of life – the despair, anxiety and difficulties that we all face at times. They remind us that, when life is difficult, God is *still* in control and God *still* surrounds us, no matter the circumstance.

We are really pleased to introduce a new contributor, Caroline Fletcher, who explores the parables Jesus tells in Matthew 13. I once heard a parable described as a story that keeps you entertained at the front door while the truth sneaks in through the back window! So, whether or not you are familiar with fishing with nets, baking bread or sowing seed – or burying your money in the ground – there are profound truths hidden in these stories, offering insights into how God works and opportunities to catch a glimpse of his kingly rule on earth.

As we open the door to the scriptures this season, we pray, along with Michele D. Morrison, in her notes on hearing God's voice, that we will be encouraged to listen expectantly, alert to his voice and enjoying his presence.

Psalms of lament and thanksgiving

Chris Leonard writes:

How are your emotions? No matter what circumstances you find yourself in, as a Christian you'll no doubt be overflowing with love, joy and peace, always. Right? Or do the grumps take over sometimes? Self-pity, fear, jealousy, desperation, a desire to hurt someone? Surely not!

And yet Psalms, that ancient worship songbook containing hymns which soar to the heights with praise addressed to the Lord, also expresses misery and even dark desires. The negativity, especially of the 'cursing' psalms, startles and shocks me. Even within a single psalm, emotions can jump all over the place. The psalms are far more real and less triumphalist than some of our worship in church. As we're not offered divine protection from woes, don't we need worship-vehicles through which we can tell God that we're depressed or angry, fearful or frustrated? There's nothing wrong with feeling and expressing emotion – in the gospels, we see Jesus laughing, weeping and feeling compassion and anger, just as his Father does. And if we tell him in a way that isn't exactly 'Christian', isn't that better than not telling him and instead burying our feelings, only to have them spring up in another form?

Bear in mind that, unlike much of the rest of the Bible, psalms are not always solely 'words about God' (which is the root meaning of 'theology'). They are words addressed to him by flawed individuals like us – except that they lived centuries before Jesus under a different covenant. And, in the absence of a police force, their culture demanded that they themselves avenge anyone wronging them or their families.

So what can we learn from a selection from Psalms 90—150, drawing on some of the lesser-known songs of lament, as well as of thanksgiving? They scream at me, 'Get real with God!' Plus, there's a Hebrew word running like a golden thread through most of what we'll be reading together – *to be revealed later!* Its meaning encompasses how remarkably consistent, faithful, strong and loving our God is. Most of the psalmists, despite their differing starting points – spiritually, morally and emotionally – grasp that thread, follow it and often end up reflecting more of his nature themselves. Pray that we might do the same.

Praise – and doubt

Give thanks to the Lord, for he is good; his love endures for ever. Let the redeemed of the Lord tell their story. (NIV)

Rejoice! Isn't it exciting to hear people's stories of how the Lord has redeemed, healed or gathered them, or released them from imprisonment, drug addictions, and so on? He rescues some from natural disasters, nourishes the starving and needy, and frees the oppressed. You might want to read Luke 4:16–21 for fascinating parallels with Jesus' declared agenda.

As a teenager, reading books like *God's Smuggler* (by Brother Andrew, 1964) and *The Cross and the Switchblade* (by David Wilkerson, 1970) showed me that God continues to work such miracles through 'ordinary' Christians. That expanded my faith and hope in him and, since then, I've written many books of encouraging true stories about others. Do spend a few moments today thanking God for his saving interventions in your own life, and for those true stories that you've read in scripture and else-where. Ask for opportunities to show people more of Jesus with your own stories of his goodness.

We celebrate that the Lord is good and that his love doesn't change – but there is a problem. Why aren't most refugees rescued? People still starve, endure modern slavery or rot in prison for their beliefs – and many aren't healed. Some drown in floods or in avalanches of suffering and despair. Are Christians in danger of telling only one side of the story, while the news media tells the darker side? It's easy to cherry-pick uplifting pas-sages from the psalms – they tend to be the most familiar. Other psalms challenge me; some I'm surprised to find in the Bible. We're not going to avoid these, but rather explore how they bring a range of human emo-tions before God. Meanwhile, look particularly at verses 1, 8, 15, 21 and 31 in this psalm. Each contains that golden thread of a Hebrew word. Can you pinpoint it?

Lord, these songs people sang to you millennia ago challenge as well as encourage us. But you are our rock and you yourself are truth. Help us grow in you as we read and pray.

CHRIS LEONARD

Gratitude and questionings

Give thanks to the Lord of lords: *His love endures for ever.* **To him who alone does great wonders,** *His love endures for ever.* **(NIV)**

The chaplain read out this psalm to a small group gathered for prayer in the prison chapel. He had explained to me about the learning difficulties and mental-health issues we might see – underlying reasons why many had ended up 'inside'. Any message we gave needed to be simple; repeating the refrain 'His love endures forever' would help it stick. Most prisoners had been used or betrayed by others, so nothing had prepared me for the joy that I saw there, and their love, kindness, honesty and inclusive spirit. I was so moved when almost all of them went on to pray their own specific thanks to God out loud – they had to be experiencing something of his transforming love. Afterwards, the chaplain said this had been an especially good day. There are setbacks but, even in that challenging situation, God's love does endure. All chaplains have to do is not get in his way!

Our key Hebrew word – it's *chesed*, often translated 'love' or 'loving kindness' – occurs 26 times in Psalm 136, expressing the strong, faithful, covenantal love of God.

But I struggle with this: can we thank God for children massacred because their obstinate ruler kept oppressing the Israelites (v. 10)? For defeating injustice, yes – that's strong, faithful and loving. But when infants and innocents suffer 'collateral damage'? Is this the psalmist's inadequate understanding of God speaking? We're told to 'give thanks in all circumstances; for this is God's will for you in Christ Jesus' (1 Thessalonians 5:18). '*In* all circumstances' may be a fine, if difficult, aim. But '*for* all circumstances'? I'm inclined neither to praise nor blame God for all the horrors we see on the news, even if those horrors are done for seemingly good reasons, such as wars of humanitarian intervention. Rather, I thank him that he is always working to bring good out of evil.

Lord, it's so good to give thanks to you, for you are good and powerful, creative and loving and you do save us. But when we have questions, help us to seek you in honesty and humility.

CHRIS LEONARD

Blame someone else?

Our tormentors demanded songs of joy… How can we sing the songs of the Lord while in a foreign land? (NIV)

This heart-rending lament, which was set to a strangely jaunty tune by Boney M ('Rivers of Babylon') and a suitably doleful one by William Walton ('Belshazzar's Feast'), concerns refugees who had been conquered and forcibly deported from their land and from their religion's central place of worship – how terrible! No wonder they're not expressing thanks to God. But maybe they should have been. The prophets had warned them time and time again what would result from their constant breaking of the special agreement, or covenant, between them and God. Finally, only this punishment of exile would cause his people to repent, resulting in their relationship with him being rekindled to life and health again, allowing his *chesed* (strong, faithful, covenantal love) to flow.

How sad that they seem more upset about the ruin of a place – Jerusalem – than the fact that they had wrecked their covenant relationship with God! I see no worship here, and no repentance either. The Babylonians didn't treat the people badly, as these things go. Prophets called the Babylonians God's agents, yet this psalmist saw them as evil, deserving of terrible punishments, such as having their infants seized and dashed against the rocks (v. 9). Really? The psalmist is yet to learn that God practises restorative, not retributive, justice. In this heart-rending psalm, surely it's God's heart that is rent.

It's easy to blame others, hurling our anger against them, when some dire situation in which we find ourselves is of our own making. We need wisdom, humility and obedience to see when God is using this to draw our attention back to him. Then he can love us back to life and health again.

But disasters also befall innocent adults and children who are powerless against the wickedness of their rulers. God's heart must break to see today's refugees.

Pray for refugees, exiles and persecuted Christians – many do continue to sing the songs of the Lord. Pray for those practising difficult restorative justice. Pray that any present or future troubles will draw you closer to God.

CHRIS LEONARD

Cursing

May no one extend kindness to him or take pity on his fatherless children. May his descendants be cut off, their names blotted out from the next generation. May the iniquity of his fathers... always remain before the Lord, that he may blot out their name from the earth. (NIV)

What a quote to read in Bible notes! Is it even in the Bible? Yes, it is, though I've never seen writing or heard preaching about it. Although I may complain that the worship songs we sing lack the emotional range of the psalms, I wouldn't want something like this included. It's written by David – the best king Israel ever had, a 'man after God's heart', often compassionate and courageous and a gifted worship leader. Ah, but he had his ups and downs, was human, had enemies. Jesus hadn't yet uttered his astounding command that we are to love our enemies and pray for those who persecute us (Matthew 5:43–44). Nor had David read Proverbs 25:21–22 (which Paul also quotes in Romans 12): 'If your enemy is hungry, give him food to eat; if he is thirsty, give him water to drink. In doing this, you will heap burning coals on his head, and the Lord will reward you.'

If God doesn't want us cursing anyone, what's Psalm 109 doing in scripture? Well, David takes his anger to God, rather than blotting out his enemy's family himself. Then, as he talks to God, his attitude changes. Although the word *chesed* appears only in verse 26 – and David wants it only for himself – he does acknowledge his desperate need of God's healing for his wounded heart.

We'll see more progress in some of David's shorter psalms. Meanwhile, what can we learn? Perhaps we can learn how important it is to look at truth as portrayed in scripture as a whole, rather than taking one passage alone. Perhaps we can learn that we should trust God for any revenge and vindication. We can say anything to him and can hand him our anger, fear and desire for revenge. He can take it and then transform us – but first, communicate!

Lord, when we feel aggrieved and angry, help us to be not afraid to talk to you honestly and to ask for your help, both with the situation and with our own reactions to it.

CHRIS LEONARD

Fear, desperation, betrayal

When my spirit grows faint within me, it is you who watch over my way. In the path where I walk people have hidden a snare for me... I have no refuge; no one cares for my life. (NIV)

Panic not, these three psalms total only 32 verses of David's lamentations and curses! He was in desperate need; King Saul was trying to have him killed. David hid in a cave with a small band of outlaws. He was constantly in fear of his life, with no sign of God's promises being fulfilled, so it is little wonder that David wants his arrogant, violent enemies obliterated. But soon he's thirsting for God, even saying, 'I hide myself in you. Teach me to do your will, for you are my God; may your good Spirit lead me on level ground' (143:9–10). (Our word *chesed* appears in 143:8, 12.)

Of course, David's enemies were also the Lord's enemies. God still hates arrogance, violence, slander and entrapment but, should he call you to join his fight against slavery or people-trafficking, domestic or sexual violence, or violent gang and drug culture, remember it's not a battle against flesh and blood but rather a spiritual battle against evil.

I enjoy the TV series *Father Brown*, about an amateur detective priest. It bears scant resemblance to the G.K. Chesterton stories on which it is based, except that, whenever a cornered criminal attacks Father Brown, the priest is empowered by being more concerned for the soul of the guilty person than for his own life. His declaration of something like 'God made you better than that' nudges them towards more than justice – some characters find repentance and salvation.

It's instinctive, perhaps, to meet violence with violence, or to respond to it by fleeing or cursing – but Jesus prayed, 'Father, forgive them, for they do not know what they are doing' (Luke 23:34). I was talking to someone who prays regularly for persecuted Christians. She said, 'I'm so humbled that they pray for those who take everything from them and their families. Jesus' way is so distinctive!'

As you talk to the Lord about those evil things that make you angry or fearful, pray with David, 'Show me the way I should go, for to you I entrust my life' (Psalm 143:8).

CHRIS LEONARD

Rooted in steadfast love

The Lord has chastened me severely, but he has not given me over to death. Open for me the gates of the righteous; I will enter and give thanks to the Lord. (NIV)

Some classify psalms for 'individual' or 'community' use. This one appears to be both, which is fine – in public worship, we often sing 'I' together, affirming we're of one mind and voice. I love the way Psalm 118 starts and ends with that constant which we keep meeting: God is love and he is good, always. Hallelujah! It's bedrock. All 'tribes' and individuals of faith can declare that as true, no matter how we feel at the time. And that's our key! The word *chesed* appears in verses 1–4 and 29, its rich meaning combining strength, steadfastness and love at the very least; then add generosity, grace, goodness, mercy and faithfulness – all of which are included in our covenant relationship.

This psalmist has a mature approach: he trusts in God through difficulties and dangers, thirsts for him and for righteousness, knows God's 'chastening' is for his good, and wills himself to keep following, worshipping and proclaiming the Lord's saving grace to others.

Where do you see Jesus in this psalm? Might he be the 'gates of the righteous' through which we enter into God's presence and kingdom (vv. 19–21)? He's certainly the stone which the builders rejected that has become the cornerstone (v. 22). The cornerstone of the new temple is his body, sacrificed 'once for all' (Hebrews 10:10). The temple includes you and me as 'living stones'. Praise him for this new way, this new gate, this new covenant and this new people, all bound together in his strong, steadfast *chesed* love.

There is so much in this psalm. What stands out for you? Talk to God about it.

Have you emerged from difficulties into a 'spacious place' (v. 5)? Thank him. Are you worried or fearful? Speak out your trust in God. Chastened? Reaffirm your desire for his ways. Suffering? Ask for new life so you can give him glory.
CHRIS LEONARD

Being blessed

When I called, you answered me; you greatly emboldened me… Your love, Lord, endures for ever – do not abandon the works of your hands. (NIV)

I read this paean of praise and thankfulness for God's faithfulness, then thought of the ups and downs of David's life and went on to read the next psalm, Psalm 139, which must be among the best-known and loved of all psalms. But Psalm 138 is also a treasure and reminds me of the beatitudes. 'Blessed are the meek' for the Lord has 'emboldened' them. Matthew 5:5 actually says the meek 'will inherit the earth'; we see an example in shepherd-boy David, as, early in his story, he is emboldened to challenge Goliath and later is raised up to reign in Jerusalem.

Naturally timid, I think other people can do most things much better than I can. I'm in need of much divine 'emboldening' before the Lord can bless others through me. If you're similar, give him thanks now!

The pure in heart 'will see God' says Matthew 5:8. The Lord, though 'lofty' and 'exalted', 'looks kindly on the lowly', says Psalm 138 – albeit 'from afar'. Under the old covenant, most 'ordinary' people had a less intimate relationship with God than we enjoy under the new, making David's knowing and being known in Psalm 139 exceptional. Thank God that, through what Jesus achieved on the cross, we each can see and know so much of God. We have infinitely more to discover when all that now obscures him from us is cleared away in the age to come!

Those who are persecuted, slandered or insulted are blessed with the kingdom of heaven, says Matthew 5:11–12. David is vindicated, preserved, saved and answered by God and his response is thankfulness and praise for the faithful love of God towards him (that word *chesed* again). I love the way David affirms the truth of that, yet doesn't take it for granted as his personal right.

Dear Lord, you bless us daily. Help us not to forget to thank, praise and glorify you. Help us also not to treat you as our personal wish-granter-cum-emergency-rescue-service.

CHRIS LEONARD

Transforming

How good it is to sing praises to our God, how pleasant and fitting to praise him!… He determines the number of the stars and calls them each by name. (NIV)

It's indeed good, fitting and pleasant to praise and thank God. He deserves it, and worship strengthens our hope and faith in him and our love for him. The psalmist reaffirms that 'the Lord delights in those who fear him, who put their faith in his unfailing love' (v. 11; *chesed* – 'loving kindness' – again). That's good to know. There are so many things to praise and thank him for in this psalm; read it again slowly, offering your own specific thanks and praises to him.

I confess that my old NIV always distracts me and makes me smile at verse 10, which says, 'His delight [is not] in the legs of a man'. The latest version clarifies the meaning, if reducing the humour, by substituting 'warrior' for 'man'. But, to be serious, let's ask again: what more might our thanks and praises do? I've been so touched by the Hillsong hymn 'So Will I (100 Billion X)'. Find this gem on YouTube or read its lyrics on **hillsong. com**. It's a brilliant 'psalm', written in 2017 in the best kind of poetry – the kind that wakes us up to grasp new things. It says that as we see and appreciate more of all God has made and done, the closer we'll be to him in our thinking, motivation, attitude and actions.

Phrases in today's psalm also wake me up. I can think of and praise the Lord for times when he has granted 'peace to [my] borders' (v. 14) and strengthened 'the bars of [my] gates' (v. 13). Is he calling us to pray for or help others whose boundaries are disputed in some way or who are vulnerable to harm? If not for nations, then perhaps we can pray for individuals or families we know.

Thank you, Lord, for making our praises and thanksgiving become transformative joy-bringers. Thank you for songs written in every age which help people to praise and to better understand who you are.

CHRIS LEONARD

After damaging stress

Return to your rest, my soul, for the Lord has been good to you. For you, Lord, have delivered me from death, my eyes from tears, my feet from stumbling, that I may walk before the Lord in the land of the living. (NIV)

I've never experienced post-traumatic stress, thank God, but it sounds to me as though the writer of Psalm 116 is just coming out of something very much like it. He speaks of the 'anguish of the grave', of being 'overcome by distress and sorrow' and of shouting, 'Lord, save me!' (vv. 3–4). It must be hard for someone, once danger and obvious extreme need have passed, to return to their normal state, where they are able to rest, trust or even be grateful.

I guess with many forms of stress reaching epidemic levels these days, the likelihood is that most of us will experience its after-effects in some form or other. I did once reach a mental state which frightened me, depriving me of sleep. It followed a few years in which one stressful set of circumstances followed hard upon another.

Once the sources of stress are gone, how might we be restored? Psalm 116 gives us some clues: first and foremost, we need someone to hear our voice and to rely on as we go forward – the Lord! Then, allowing ourselves to be needy but without fear, we need to realise that there is hope, that we will 'walk before the Lord' (v. 9) again. We can ask for help – from him and perhaps a wise Christian friend. We can tell our souls to be at rest because God has been good to us.

Thankfulness is key – write down any little thing you're thankful for, even if you can't 'pray' it. Another key is taking some moments to still yourself before him each day and simply 'be'. He loves you as you are; even if you feel like death, you're precious to him and his love is strong enough to free you from the 'chains' of whatever you're enduring, and to build you up to live free and strong again!

Lord, thank you that the ancient wisdom in this psalm works for our stress-filled age. Even when we feel like failures, utterly defeated, flattened and frightened, you don't change. Your strong, compassionate love never fails.

CHRIS LEONARD

In the depths – hope!

Out of the depths I cry to you, Lord; Lord, hear my voice. Let your ears be attentive to my cry for mercy… Israel, put your hope in the Lord, for with the Lord is unfailing love and with him is full redemption. (NIV)

This is one of the 'songs of ascents' (Psalms 120—134), sung by pilgrims approaching Jerusalem for the great feasts – and also by priests ascending the steps of the temple. The sequence in this psalm shows a kind of progress. This one is beautiful. In 'the depths', the psalmist isn't blaming God or anyone else, but asks for mercy and is confident of God's forgiveness. He's waiting for God 'more than watchmen wait for the morning' (v. 6). Many years ago, in Ghana, I was often woken by the night watchman who used to patrol around the house, singing – and I'd think of this psalm. Poor man; each night must have seemed endless.

Have you ever plummeted into the depths of despair, waiting for God in the long darkness? Just as watchmen know the night will end, so the psalmist trusts God's *chesed* (v. 7). The words 'unfailing' or 'everlasting', which so often accompany *chesed*, have their Hebrew root in the word 'eternal'. Creation was made in his *chesed* (Psalm 136:5–9) and some believe that God is redeeming us to a state of *chesed* – beyond the end of this age, we'll all live within and practise it. Imagine, not that there's no heaven, as John Lennon sang, but the bliss when that strong and stead-fast love reigns in everyone's hearts.

Meanwhile, this word runs through Psalms and more of the Old Testament like a shining thread through the dark and difficult bits. We, through Jesus, have seen a lot more of God's grace and special kind of love, but we're still waiting for full redemption and our emotions waver. My grand-daughter, aged two, swings from joy to anguish, from giggles to fury or terror, within seconds. Through it all, her parents hold her in *chesed* love, just as God holds us. She'll grow, as will you and I! Thank God!

Lord, whether we're in the depths lamenting, or soaring to the heights in praise and thanksgiving, may our hope rest in your unfailing love.

CHRIS LEONARD

Confidence at last

The righteous… will still bear fruit in old age, they will stay fresh and green, proclaiming, 'The Lord is upright; he is my Rock, and there is no wickedness in him.' (NIV)

For over a decade after I joined my current church, very few members died. However, in the last four years, there's been a thanksgiving service for the life of a much-loved church member almost every other month. It's sad, of course; these people are very much missed, but they remain a growing 'cloud of witnesses' (see Hebrews 11) to God's faithful love. With some individuals, despite years of shattered health of mind or body, the life-spark of God has always been evident, both in those caring for their loved ones and in the sufferers themselves. Then comes death: from one point of view, the worst has happened – and yet, at the funerals, outpourings of thankfulness proclaim the strength and the hope bestowed by God's faithful love. He is the Rock.

The fruit of the Spirit (love, joy, peace, patience, kindness, goodness, faithfulness, gentleness and self-control; see Galatians 5:22–23) in old age, and indeed at any age, often isn't grown without a struggle. And that's okay. We can give God our bitterness, our frustrations and fears, our selfish ambitions, our shame and sense of failure. His goodness can absorb it all, since Jesus took it all on the cross and put it to death. And then he and he alone produces the fruit in us.

It's good to sing psalms and songs of praise to the Lord when we're together in church on Sundays, at funerals and every day. It is good to make music, to exalt our wonderful Lord and to learn, as the saints have done through the ages, to flourish in him and to proclaim his goodness. And, when you're alone, why not make a practice of writing your own psalms or keeping a spiritual journal? Tell God your highs and lows. Allow him to work his transformation, and be wrapped in his *chesed*.

'It is good to praise the Lord and make music to your name, O Most High, proclaiming your love in the morning and your faithfulness at night' (vv. 1–2).

CHRIS LEONARD

John's good news reveals Jesus

Christine Platt writes:

Who is Jesus and why did he come? These are the questions which the apostle John so eloquently answers in this gospel. John 20:30–31 are foundational verses: 'Jesus provided far more God-revealing signs than are written down in this book. These are written down so you will believe that Jesus is the Messiah, the Son of God, and in the act of believing, have real and eternal life in the way he personally revealed it' (MSG). One of the key words is 'revealed'.

John wants to reveal Jesus to us in all his wonder, not merely to inform our minds but to enable us to believe and receive eternal life, which is to know God (John 17:3). John is utterly determined to make sure we don't miss anything that could help us understand and believe. He has carefully selected stories, teachings and experiences which introduce us to different facets of our Saviour Jesus.

John was a young man when he first met Jesus and responded to his call to follow him (Mark 1:19–20). John and his brother James worked with their father, Zebedee, in the family fishing business. John was close to Jesus throughout the three years of his earthly ministry and is therefore well-placed to give us an accurate account of what it was like to live alongside God in human form, as astounding as that sounds.

As well as this gospel, John also wrote three letters and the book of Revelation. Unlike some of the other apostles, he lived a long life. He served in the early church and especially ministered to the church in Ephesus. Ninety per cent of his gospel is unique to John and not also contained in Matthew, Mark or Luke, so we are deeply indebted to John for this additional material.

It is most probable that John wrote his gospel after the others had been circulated. We can imagine him in older age, reflecting on those incredible three years and all that had happened since. His years of service, study and learning to walk day by day with God gave him a rich depth of understanding, which he poured out in his gospel. Let's learn from this wise, godly man, who had a front-row seat during the most pivotal time in human history.

Who is he?

In the beginning the Word already existed… the Word was God… God created everything through him… The Word gave life to everything that was created, and his life brought light to everyone. The light shines in the darkness, and the darkness can never extinguish it. (NLT)

The identity of Jesus is the fundamental question we all have to get to grips with. Our understanding of who he is will affect every moment of our lives.

Here, John echoes the early chapters of Genesis, where God spoke creation into being. God said: 'Let there be…' and it happened – sky, sea, land, animals, birds and people appeared! In his gospel, John declares that God through Jesus spoke salvation into being. He is creator. He is light. He brings life. Jesus is God, not merely a prophet, nor even an exceptionally good man, nor the mightiest angel. He is God himself. 'The Word became human and made his home among us' (v. 14).

We are perhaps more used to thinking of Jesus as 'one of us', as indeed he was, whereas maybe we see God the Father as more distant, unapproachable, more 'other', sometimes a bit scary. We need to expand our minds to grasp the reality that in Jesus, the unapproachable 'other' became 'one of us'. 'No one has ever seen God. But the unique One, who is himself God, is near to the Father's heart. He has revealed God to us' (v. 18).

Even as I write this, I'm struggling to get my head around it: the God who put the universe in place reduced himself to fit into a fragile human envelope and came to a broken, unbelieving people to show us what God was like: 'full of unfailing love and faithfulness' (v. 14). He endured rejection and murder to be the light that shines in the darkness which the darkness could never extinguish.

How do you see Jesus on this continuum from holy, awesome God to your best friend? What can you do to bring these two truths closer together?

Holy, magnificent Jesus, King of kings and Lord of lords, I worship you today. Help me understand more about you. Thank you that you are my friend and that you love me.

CHRISTINE PLATT

Revealing Jesus

The next day John saw Jesus coming towards him and said, 'Look, the Lamb of God, who takes away the sin of the world! This is the one I meant when I said, "A man who comes after me has surpassed me because he was before me."' (NIV)

Have you ever had to introduce a guest speaker to an audience? You have to get the facts right and aim to inspire the audience to listen carefully to what the speaker has to say. This was John the Baptist's job. (He was a different John to the gospel writer.) His role was to get people ready to listen to Jesus. That involved showing them that their relationship with God was broken and offering them the baptism of repentance – the sign that they realised they had gone the wrong way and were determined to turn around and follow God.

John made it abundantly clear that he himself was not the main act. He deliberately didn't steal the limelight. Several times in this passage, he puts Jesus ahead of himself – for example, 'He was before me' (v. 30); 'I am not worthy to untie [his sandals]' (v. 27). For John, Jesus was definitely the star of the show. When two of his own followers left him to go after Jesus, he freely let them go. John's unique task was to reveal Jesus to Israel and he did it brilliantly. People were intrigued and eager to hear and see Jesus.

What can we learn from John the Baptist about revealing Jesus to people? John's lifestyle was compelling. He certainly didn't blend in. We don't all need to live in the desert, wear clothes made of camel's hair and eat locusts and wild honey (Matthew 3:4), but we do need to ask the question: is my lifestyle any different from those who don't yet know God? Would people know I love God as they observe my relationships, how I use my money and time, and my speech? Would those who observe my life see anything that intrigues them to ask questions?

Pray over this verse and ask God to speak to you about it: 'Do not conform to the pattern of this world, but be transformed by the renewing of your mind' (Romans 12:2).

CHRISTINE PLATT

First glimpses of Jesus' power

What Jesus did here in Cana of Galilee was the first of the signs through which he revealed his glory; and his disciples believed in him. (NIV)

We've seen how John the gospel writer sought to reveal Jesus to his readers through mirroring the verses in Genesis, and also how John the Baptist revealed Jesus to Israel. Now, Jesus himself begins to show the people who he is.

In the first sign – turning water into wine – Jesus rescues the wedding host from social embarrassment. When the disciples saw this, they got a glimpse of his supernatural power.

In the second sign, Jesus clears the temple area from being a market-place. Can you imagine the chaos? Sheep bleating, cattle mooing, angry traders yelling. When the disciples saw this, they began to see Jesus as the one prophesied about: 'Zeal for your house consumes me' (Psalm 69:9). Their Old Testament knowledge helped them understand.

The third sign is when Jesus is challenged by the Jewish leaders and he declares, 'Destroy this temple, and I will raise it again in three days' (v. 19). Some of Jesus' statements were quite baffling at the time. Only after his resurrection did the disciples make the connection and realise that the temple he referred to was his body.

These three incidents show us how we can understand God. Some things are clear: water into wine shows us his provision and power, and most of us can remember seeing him provide for us and for others. Some things we grasp more as we study God's word and learn about the history and culture of the times. But some things are hidden, and we will not understand them fully until we meet Jesus face to face.

As we go through John's gospel, we will see more of Jesus' character, purposes and teaching. Let's appreciate what we can understand now, and trust him for what will be revealed later.

'Open my eyes that I may see wonderful things in your law' (Psalm 119:18).

CHRISTINE PLATT

God loves everyone

For God so loved the world that he gave his one and only Son, that whoever believes in him shall not perish but have eternal life. For God did not send his Son into the world to condemn the world, but to save the world through him. (NIV)

Do you find some people easy to love and others more challenging? It's tempting to spend time with those whose personalities gel with ours, and to avoid more difficult people. Take a look around at your next Christian gathering and see who's being left out in the cold. This is not God's way.

In these passages, we see Jesus interacting with two very different people – a questioning intellectual man and a foreign woman with a shady background. Yet he treats both of them with dignity and takes their questions seriously. In short, he shows God's love to them. Merely talking with a Samaritan woman was frowned upon for Jewish men – Jesus' disciples were shocked.

Jesus broke several cultural barriers in relation to this Samaritan. We also might find it necessary to break cultural barriers at times. Certainly, we will need to tip ourselves out of our comfort zones to make the message of Jesus' love visible to the watching world.

Of all the attributes of God that Jesus came to reveal, love is the biggie. When God's love is clearly demonstrated, the world sits up and takes notice. Mother Teresa is almost universally admired for her devoted care to the poorest of the poor. She referred to them as 'Jesus in his distressing disguise'. That's the motivation of her compassionate heart: when she was serving them, she was serving Jesus.

If God has given you friends who are fun and enjoyable, rejoice! But also take the initiative with the less fun people and see them as Jesus himself. You might get a surprise at how nice these people are once you get to know them. Use this prayer of Mother Teresa and see what God will do.

Lord, though you hide yourself behind the unattractive disguises of the irritable, the exacting, the unreasonable, may I still recognise you, and say, 'Jesus, my patient, how sweet it is to serve you.'

CHRISTINE PLATT

Jesus claims God is his Father

Jesus said to them, 'My Father is always at his work… and I, too, am working.' For this reason [the Jewish leaders] tried all the more to kill him; not only was he breaking the Sabbath, but he was even calling God his own Father, making himself equal with God. (NIV)

You might have seen the poignant scene in the film *Shrek*, where the eponymous ogre blurts out, 'Onions have layers! Ogres have layers!' We all have layers. In this conversation with the Jewish leaders, Jesus peels back another layer to reveal more of himself. He declares that God is his Father, which the Jews interpret as a claim to a special relationship with God – indeed, such a close bond as to make himself equal with God. Jesus thus places himself above any other prophet or teacher.

To the Jewish mind, this was shocking blasphemy – unless, of course, it was true. Very few of the scholars and leaders even entertained that possibility. Although they diligently studied the scriptures, it did not benefit them or bring insights because their minds were rigid and closed. That is a dangerous and pitiful state to be in. We need always to be ready to listen to other viewpoints and not reject them without first examining them against scripture.

Jesus goes on to peel back another layer. Because of his close relationship with his Father, he can only act in complete dependence upon him: 'The Son can do nothing by himself; he can do only what he sees his Father doing' (v. 19). All the phenomenal miracles and teachings weren't just a demonstration of Jesus' power; they were initiated by God the Father and enacted through his Son – a glorious partnership.

Amazingly, this is a partnership to which you and I are invited to belong. Jesus prayed: 'Father, just as you are in me and I am in you. May they also be in us so that the world may believe that you have sent me' (17:21). How's your partnership going?

Thank you, Lord, that you invite me to partner with you. That's amazing!
CHRISTINE PLATT

Bread from heaven

'For the bread of God is the bread that comes down from heaven and gives life to the world.'… Then Jesus declared, 'I am the bread of life.' (NIV)

This concept of bread from heaven was of huge significance to Jewish people. It was a common expectation that, when the Messiah came, he would also distribute manna just as Moses did in the desert. Jesus points out that it wasn't Moses who gave them the bread; in reality, it came from God. Then he drops his bombshell revelation: 'I am the bread of life' (v. 35) and 'I am the bread that came down from heaven' (v. 41).

Can you imagine their confusion? They've just seen him miraculously turn five loaves into enough bread to feed 5,000 men, plus women and children. They are thinking of physical bread that nourishes their stomachs. Then he says, 'I am the bread of life.' Jesus seems to add to the mystery of it all by adding, 'This bread is my flesh, which I will give for the life of the world' (v. 51).

Those of us who know how the story unfolds realise Jesus was talking about his death and resurrection to pay for the world's sins. But to his hearers on that day, it must have sounded very strange. Many turned away from him.

I doubt Simon Peter and the other close disciples understood what he meant, but they held on in faith, even in their doubt and confusion. They trusted in what they did know: 'You have the words of eternal life. We have come to believe and to know that you are the Holy One of God' (6:68–69).

There will be times when we struggle to fathom God's ways. But we need to guard against that causing us to turn away. Instead, we need to stake our faith on what we can grasp, and trust him with our questions.

As you eat your toast or sandwich today (or even if you don't!), take time to thank Jesus for being the bread of life – for dying in your place and giving you spiritual life as well as bread to nourish your physical body.

CHRISTINE PLATT

Jesus truly understood the law

The Jews there were amazed and asked, 'How did this man get such learning without having been taught?' Jesus answered, 'My teaching is not my own. It comes from him who sent me.' (NIV)

Jesus was a superb teacher. The people and even hard-boiled soldiers were highly impressed with him. In these passages, we see Jesus tackling two big issues – the laws about the sabbath and the laws about adultery. In both cases, he reveals God's true intent for the law.

The religious leaders had stifled the sabbath day of rest with restrictive rules and regulations. Even today, in some hotels in Israel, a lift is set aside for Jewish people on the sabbath which stops at every floor so that devout Jews don't have to 'work', i.e. press a button. How sad. God's plan for the sabbath was joy, rest, refreshment and worship. Jesus healed a man on the sabbath (John 5). He broke man-made rules but honoured God's intent.

In the case of this unfortunate woman caught in adultery (notice the man was nowhere to be seen!), Jesus saw through the crowd's machinations. He made them acknowledge their own guilt, which then gave them no right to accuse this woman. They'd come with such self-righteous anger, aiming to catch Jesus out and to punish this terrified woman. It must have been galling to slink away shamefaced. After they left, Jesus spoke gently to her and showed mercy, but also urged her to change her ways. Again, he revealed God's true intent.

How much we need wisdom and discernment as we read God's word, so that we don't go off on a tangent and construct a whole theology out of one verse taken out of context! Fortunately, we are not left to our own devices. Jesus also makes an oblique reference to the Holy Spirit (7:38–39), who is now our teacher and guide.

'But the Advocate, the Holy Spirit, whom the Father will send in my name, will teach you all things and will remind you of everything I have said to you' (John 14:26). Thank God for his counsellor.

CHRISTINE PLATT

The world's light

Jesus then said, 'I came into the world to bring everything into the clear light of day, making all the distinctions clear, so that those who have never seen will see, and those who have made a great pretense of seeing will be exposed as blind.' (MSG)

I've recently had cataract surgery so, for the first time since primary school, I can see without specs! I identify in a small way with this man born blind to whom Jesus gave the gift of sight.

Jesus uses this healing of physical blindness to illustrate the need for healing of spiritual blindness, which is far more serious. The man was healed both physically and spiritually – possibly all on the same day. What a transformation!

Jesus still is the world's light. He came in human form 2,000 years ago but he still is the answer to the world's spiritual blindness. He came 'to bring everything into the clear light of day, making all the distinctions clear, so that those who have never seen will see' (v. 39). Do you know people like that? People who rarely if ever think about God, the meaning of life or what happens when we die? Jesus still comes today for them.

He also comes for 'those who have made a great pretense of seeing [and who] will be exposed as blind' (v. 39). Many of the religious teachers in Jesus' day took overweening pride in their knowledge but had still gone drastically off track. Do you know any people like that? People who think they've got life sorted out and pour scorn on anyone else's ideas? Jesus wants to bring light to them, too.

I'm often tempted to give up on some people who seem determined to stumble around in the darkness of their own making. This image of Jesus as the light reminds me that there is always hope. Even if they don't want to listen to me, I can still pray – and in God's time, light will dawn.

In your charitable giving, consider contributing towards medical missions which bring sight to the blind. Pray that, in their physical healing, people will also receive spiritual healing.

CHRISTINE PLATT

Good shepherd

**'I am the good shepherd; I know my sheep and my sheep know me…
and I lay down my life for the sheep.' (NIV)**

I recently watched a sheep-farming programme on TV. The farmer had a sizeable flock and he looked after the sheep well. Some of what the farmer did may have been surprising and disturbing to the sheep. He dosed them for worms, sheared them and used dogs to move them around different fields. The aim was to keep them healthy.

Similarly, some things that our good shepherd allows in our lives may be uncomfortable and incomprehensible. In all these events, the key factor to remember is that our shepherd is good and works for our welfare. He does know best.

Sometimes, a foolish sheep runs away from its shepherd. It's also tempting for us to wander off and look for more enticing pastures elsewhere. The alternative to sticking with our good shepherd is to fall into the clutches of the thief – the enemy whose desire is to 'steal and kill and destroy' (v. 10). Our good shepherd promises us life 'to the full'. Even when events baffle us, we need to look to our shepherd and remember his character of goodness, and also remind ourselves of how he has led us in the past. Even though we may have gone through some dark times, he has led us through into the sunshine and we are richer for the experience.

Maybe you're in a dark valley or barren desert right now. Jesus hasn't changed. He is still the good shepherd who has positive plans for you: 'plans to prosper you and not to harm you, plans to give you hope and a future' (Jeremiah 29:11). Jesus went through his darkest hour so that you and I could have life to the full. He is the faithful shepherd, who is worth hanging on to no matter what comes our way.

'The Lord is my shepherd, I lack nothing' (Psalm 23:1). Thank you, Jesus, for your promise. I choose to trust you in all the events of this day, whether they are pleasant or not.

CHRISTINE PLATT

Power over death

Jesus called in a loud voice, 'Lazarus, come out!' The dead man came out, his hands and feet wrapped with strips of linen, and a cloth round his face. Jesus said to them, 'Take off the grave clothes and let him go.' (NIV)

The pace is hotting up. Jesus was preparing for the crescendo of his life. This God-revealing act of triumph over death caused many to believe in him. Others, the religious leaders, decided it was the last straw. They stubbornly made more deliberate plans to kill Jesus. Even though they acknowledged the reality of the miracle, they were more concerned about losing prestige and power than entertaining the possibility that Jesus came from God. They were blinded by pride and fear.

The raising of Lazarus foreshadowed the more earth- and heaven-shattering miracle of Jesus rising from the dead. Lazarus would eventually die and stay physically dead. Jesus is alive now and forever! In his death and resurrection, he destroyed 'him who holds the power of death – that is, the devil' (Hebrews 2:14).

The attempts of the Jewish religious leaders to kill off Jesus were a tiny sideshow to what was really happening in the spiritual realm. In that glorious scene of holy sacrifice on the cross and then the empty tomb, Satan was stripped of his power. Now what we experience are Satan's last lingering attempts to turn us away from God. He knows he hasn't got long. His end will surely come. In Revelation 12:12, John explains further: '[Satan] is filled with fury, because he knows that his time is short.' We face a defeated, limping enemy.

It was with complete confidence that Jesus could say, 'I am the resurrection and the life. The one who believes in me will live, even though they die; and whoever lives by believing in me will never die' (John 11:25–26). Jesus today asks us the same question he asked Martha: 'Do you believe this?'

Do you believe this? Do your friends and family believe this? Ask God for opportunities to pass on your faith to others.

CHRISTINE PLATT

Life through death

'Unless a grain of wheat falls to the ground and dies, it remains only a single seed. But if it dies, it produces many seeds… Now my soul is troubled, and what shall I say? "Father, save me from this hour?" No, it was for this very reason I came.' (NIV)

Here, Jesus is revealing to his disciples, his friends and the crowd God's magnificent plan to bring eternal salvation to all people, both Jews and Gentiles. The crowd expected him to seize earthly power, send the Romans packing and reign over a renewed Jewish nation. Wrong!

The imagery of life through death is evident in the natural world. How disappointing it is when we plant seeds with great anticipation and nothing seems to happen. The seed looks dead, tucked underground, but is actually secretly carrying out its purpose.

Jesus had to die physically to fulfil his destiny. Yet he must have died to himself every day of his earthly life. Many courageous believers risk death and some are martyred for their faith. For most of us, however, dying to self involves a daily decision to put God and others first and not to cling to our supposed rights and preferences. The paradox is that, if we concentrate on personal fulfilment and success, we will lose what is most important. We may enjoy worldly acclaim, but that doesn't bring us closer to God. Jesus could have had the world bowing at his feet, but he chose the way of humiliation, suffering and ultimately death.

Mary's costly offering to Jesus (v. 3) illustrates the depth of her love. That perfume may well have been her dowry or her provision for later life. She poured it all out. I find that so challenging. I think I might have been tempted to keep half of the perfume. She was criticised for that lavish gesture, but Jesus commended her. We won't always be understood by others when we put God first, but Jesus will approve.

Lord Jesus, thank you for your life of self-denial. Help me today to follow your example. Not my will, but yours be done. Keep me attentive to your Spirit's invitation to put you and others first.

CHRISTINE PLATT

The Father's gift

'I will talk to the Father, and he'll provide you another Friend so that you will always have someone with you. This Friend is the Spirit of Truth… I will not leave you orphaned.' (MSG)

Jesus now reveals another astounding part of God's plan. He had already warned his friends several times that he was going to be killed. They had witnessed growing threats from the religious leaders. Naturally, they were anxious, scared and bewildered. What would life be like without Jesus? He was their friend, their teacher, the one they pinned their hopes on and soon, it seemed, he would be gone. What would they do without him in their lives?

Jesus understood their panic and reassured them. He wasn't going to abandon them but would send a friend, a counsellor, the Holy Spirit to always be with them. This friend would not be limited to a physical body like Jesus was in his earthly life, but would be 'in them'.

Jesus' parting gift was 'peace. I don't leave you the way you're used to being left – feeling abandoned, bereft. So don't be upset. Don't be distraught' (v. 27). How desperately the disciples would need that gift of peace over the coming days. Jesus gives us the same promise of peace today and sometimes it's just as hard to believe it and to live it out.

The Holy Spirit's role was to make everything plain to them. He would remind them of all the things Jesus had told them. When the Holy Spirit came at Pentecost (Acts 2:1–4), Jesus' followers were changed people – full of confidence, joy and trust – and many others believed through their message (2:41).

We have the same Holy Spirit who wants to be in us, to teach us and to empower us for all the challenges that we face today. If you're finding it hard to hold on to peace, the Holy Spirit is your helper.

Ask the Holy Spirit to calm your heart and mind. It can be a tough struggle because the 'chief of this godless world' (v. 30) will try to derail us – just as he tried to with Jesus.

CHRISTINE PLATT

King of the Jews

'Here is your king,' Pilate said to the Jews. But they shouted, 'Take him away! Take him away! Crucify him!' 'Shall I crucify your king?' Pilate asked. 'We have no king but Caesar,' the chief priests answered. (NIV)

The Roman soldiers, the Jewish leaders and Pilate, as well as the crowd, should have fallen to their knees and worshipped Jesus in adoration. Instead, the soldiers in mockery dressed him up like a king (John 19:1–3). The chief priests were so obsessed with having him killed that they denied their reason for living. They were supposed to lead the Jewish nation in worship of God, but they claimed the despised Roman emperor as their king! What were they thinking? Pilate treated Jesus as a common criminal, despite knowing he was innocent. Most of the crowd yelled for his blood.

The tragic irony in this episode beggars belief. Their king and Messiah hangs dying on a cross which states clearly that he is the king of the Jews. The crime of the accused was often fixed to the cross. Jesus was the one who bowed his head so that their and our heads could be lifted high. He was stripped and covered in blood and spit so that they and we could be clothed with his purity. 'For he has clothed me with garments of salvation and arrayed me in a robe of his righteousness' (Isaiah 61:10). But they rejected him.

Into this horror, John inserts a poignant detail which reveals the compassionate and tender heart of Jesus. In his agony, Jesus looked down and saw his sorrowing mother with John standing nearby. The sight of these two must have so comforted his heart. He entrusted his mother to John's care.

Later, Joseph of Arimathea and Nicodemus played their part in giving honour to Jesus' body as the king that he was – by giving him a dignified and beautiful burial.

King Jesus, I worship you this day. Thank you for the unimaginable price you paid so I could be covered with your purity and holiness. I dedicate myself to serve you as my king.

CHRISTINE PLATT

Breakfast with Jesus

Jesus said to them, 'Bring some of the fish you have just caught.' So Simon Peter climbed back into the boat and dragged the net ashore. It was full of large fish, 153, but even with so many the net was not torn. Jesus said to them, 'Come and have breakfast.' (NIV)

Four years ago, I had the inspiring adventure of visiting Israel. We went to Tabgha by the Sea of Galilee – the traditional site where Jesus cooked breakfast for his disciples. This event came alive for me in a new way as I walked along this stretch of beach. I could picture that group of men sharing bread and fish in a relaxed yet awestruck atmosphere. The disciples knew Jesus had come alive again. They had already seen him twice. What must it have been like to share this simple meal with him?

For Peter, this was probably the most significant meal of his life. I wonder how much his abandonment and denial of Jesus still cast deep sadness and shame over him. Jesus gives Peter the opportunity to confess his love. Gone is the brash Peter who boasted he would die with Jesus. Now he admits that Jesus knows everything, even the depths of Peter's heart (v. 17). He doesn't claim any knowledge or macho greatness for himself.

This breakfast on the beach shows us that Jesus knows our physical and emotional needs. The disciples had been fishing and had caught nothing. Jesus provided a monster catch for them. They were hungry and probably cold, so he built a fire and cooked fish and bread. The fire of coals would have reminded Peter of the time he warmed himself at a fire when he denied Jesus. Jesus reinstated and reaffirmed Peter and set him back on his feet. The environment was peaceful, friendly and holy.

Jesus promises to meet our needs and we don't need to beg or plead. He knows where we are at. We just need to respond to his invitation: 'Come, have breakfast and follow me.'

'And my God will meet all your needs according to his riches of his glory in Christ Jesus' (Philippians 4:19). Claim this promise for today and respond to Jesus' invitation to come and follow.

CHRISTINE PLATT

A handful of kings

Sheila Jacobs writes:

So, when you're deciding on an interesting Bible-reading exercise, do you ever think, 'Hey! I'll study the kings of Judah'? No? Well, prepare to be challenged!

The books of Kings are one long story, divided into two. They chart the impressive and not-so-impressive rise and fall of many individuals who led God's people, following on from King David and his son Solomon. The books of Chronicles, probably written after the Babylonian captivity, provide another intriguing insight into the same time period.

Solomon started off well: the kingdom of Israel had become united under Saul and David, but it prospered under Solomon. The Lord appeared to Solomon in a dream and told him he could ask for anything. Solomon asked for wisdom to rule God's people and was given that and much more besides. He built the magnificent temple and, when he had finished building that and his palace, the Lord appeared to him again. If you have time, read through his story (1 Kings 2—11); it sets the scene for what is to come. Especially take note of his wonderful prayer in 1 Kings 8.

Unfortunately, although Solomon started well, he ended badly. God is a covenant God. Solomon broke the covenant. He walked away from his King. He married wives who worshipped other gods, and it seems that, under their influence, he did too. Because of this, God warned him that he would tear most of the kingdom away from him – but not during his lifetime. That's how Israel became a divided kingdom, with ten tribes in the north, and Judah and Benjamin under the rule of Solomon's descendants in the south.

In these notes, we will be looking at some of the kings who led Judah, its capital being Jerusalem. We are unable to cover them all, or the amazing prophets of this time, or look at the period in any historical depth. Instead, we'll explore the lives of these long-ago leaders and think about what we can learn from them. How does this portion of the word of God impact us today?

Some kings were good; some weren't. Some loved God and made mistakes, just like us. Before you start reading, I suggest you ask God to reveal what he is saying to you, in your situation. I hope you will be blessed, encouraged, inspired – and, yes, challenged!

The wrong counsel

But Rehoboam rejected the advice the elders gave him and consulted the young men who had grown up with him and were serving him. (NIV)

God's words have come true; the kingdom is divided. Jeroboam, 'one of Solomon's officials' (1 Kings 11:26), rebelled against Solomon and fled to Egypt. Now Solomon is dead, Jeroboam returns. There is discontent in the kingdom due to Solomon's substantial taxation, described here as 'a heavy yoke' (v. 4). It's interesting to note that the glorious rule of Solomon ended in such a way. But Solomon had clearly walked away from God. Because he was their ruler, this would have had a huge impact on his people.

Rehoboam, his son, has to face the discontent – and the rebel leader. So what does he do? Ask for wisdom from trusted elders? No. He goes to the young guys he hangs out with and they give him absolutely the wrong advice. Instead of a kind, servant-hearted answer, he gives the people a harsh reply. And he pays the price. Verse 16 effectively tells us that those who were not of David's tribe immediately turned away from the rule of David's dynasty.

And so we have the sorry sight of a once-prosperous nation divided. Who knows what might have been the outcome if Rehoboam had sought God, repented and behaved as wisely as his father had done at first?

There are always consequences when we turn away from the Lord. And there are times when we seem only too eager to seek the counsel of those who will endorse what we want to do, rather than what we know God wants us to do.

If this is you, today, find someone you trust who will tell you the truth. Seek out wise counsel, even if you know that person will tell you something you don't want to hear. Feelings lie. The word of God doesn't. Choose life, not death.

Are you a leader? Do you take wise counsel? How might it impact those you are leading if you listen to the wrong voice? Pray for God's guidance, wisdom and protection.

SHEILA JACOBS

We rely on you

Then Asa called to the Lord his God and said, 'Lord, there is no one like you to help the powerless against the mighty. Help us, Lord our God, for we rely on you.' (NIV)

I love this prayer! King Asa, who did 'what was good and right in the eyes of the Lord' (v. 2), knows where to go and what to do when trouble hits. Faced with a mighty enemy, he calls out to God and declares his reliance upon him.

There are times in my life when I have felt totally powerless. When I was younger, I became very ill. At that time, I also lost my job and a long-term relationship ended – all within about eight months. I remember sitting by the fire feeling bewildered. All I had wanted to do was work for God, and now I could do nothing except take my dog for walks, when I felt well enough. But in that time of utter dependence on God, I realised that, although I had wanted to 'work for' him, he wanted to do his work in and through me. I had to learn to 'let go and let God'. Reading Watchman Nee's *Sit, Walk, Stand* (1957) helped, as I began to understand that we need to rest in order to move in God. But letting go of something we cherish – hopes, dreams, even relationships – isn't easy.

Naturally, I think we all like to be in control – or believe we are. I know I do! But countless times since I was unwell, I have realised that it's a fallacy to think I actually control anything. However, there is one who is bigger than me, who loves me and on whom I can truly rely; one who tells me to trust and not fear, to obey and to follow.

God has a good plan for us and we need to surrender to him. As we do, we'll walk on the path he has chosen for us.

Dear Father, I often feel so powerless. But I know that you ask me to rely fully on you. Help me to step out in faith today, knowing that all will be well, because you are with me.

SHEILA JACOBS

Follow that leader?

Then he assembled all Judah and Benjamin and the people from Ephraim, Manasseh and Simeon who had settled among them, for large numbers had come over to him from Israel when they saw that the Lord his God was with him. (NIV)

Asa's 'heart was fully committed to the Lord all his life' (v. 17). In today's passage, we read that, under Asa, the people enter into a covenant to seek the Lord 'with all their heart and soul' (v. 12).

Isn't it wonderful when we have leaders in our churches who are on fire for God? Or when we see an amazing preacher on the TV or the internet? It's so exciting to be around people who are 'anointed', those who seem to be specially used by God. I wonder how many people pray for a gifted leader, who is able to preach with such power that 'large numbers' come to our fellowship to hear the gospel, with signs and wonders following?

Still, we need to remember that, as much as leaders can be a blessing, it isn't about gifted people; it's about God. Asa was humble in his reliance on the Lord, as we saw in yesterday's note. He wasn't perfect, but God was present with him.

Sometimes, we may look at the people ministering rather than remembering that, although it is great to have powerful leaders, we are all works in progress. We can become disappointed when people let us down. But we're all just human – even the most 'anointed' person we know.

Let's make sure we fix our eyes on Jesus, not on people. And as we do that, let's invite others to do the same. If they are attracted to who is in us, they will want to know more about him and perhaps want to follow him. Jesus is the one who draws people to himself (John 12:32). If we want to make real, genuine disciples, we need to be like Asa – humbly admitting our reliance on God, focusing on him.

Lord, help me today to fix my eyes just on you. And as I do that, I know that your sweetness will leak out to others. Thank you, Jesus.

SHEILA JACOBS

Seeking God

The Lord was with Jehoshaphat because he followed the ways of his father David before him. He did not consult the Baals but sought the God of his father and followed his commands rather than the practices of Israel. (NIV)

Jehoshaphat, the son of Asa, starts well – and unlike his ancestor Solomon, finishes well too – although he makes a big mistake along the way, as we will see in a later note.

It's so easy to start our life as disciples full of good intentions. But as we go on, we discover there are valleys and hills to negotiate in the journey of following Jesus. There are also distractions. Sometimes we are tempted to switch our focus, as we become preoccupied with stuff. We may not view it as idolatry, but whatever occupies our minds and hearts can swiftly take the place of God.

It's interesting to read above that God is with Jehoshaphat because he follows the ways of David – wholehearted devotion – not consulting other 'gods' but seeking the Lord and obeying his commands.

What does it mean to seek the Lord? It's about spending time with him, getting to know him through his word and through prayer. We are loved and highly valued. It's not about 'works'; it's about relationship.

The more time we spend with someone, the better we know them. The more time we spend with Jesus, the better we will be able to discern his voice (see John 10:2–5). 'Growing in knowing', we will follow him more closely.

How much time do you spend with God? Do you find you are easily distracted? Focusing on other stuff can blur our vision of reality. Is there something you can put down in favour of seeking God's presence, spending time with Jesus? If you find that your walk with Jesus is no longer the main focus of your life, is it time to stop awhile and reassess your journey?

Father, please enable me to set aside the good things you have blessed me with in order to spend time with the giver. Help me to be aware of what distracts, and to listen to you.

SHEILA JACOBS

Hearing the right thing

The king of Israel answered Jehoshaphat, 'There is still one prophet through whom we can enquire of the Lord, but I hate him because he never prophesies anything good about me, but always bad.' (NIV)

Here, we take a quick detour as we glance at the king of Israel, the notorious Ahab, who seeks to make an alliance with King Jehoshaphat. King Jehoshaphat encourages Ahab to seek God's counsel first. Ahab does, but he hears what the advisers clearly believe he wants to hear. However, Jehoshaphat wants to know what the Lord says. Can't you just hear the grumpy Ahab: 'Huh! Well, we could ask this guy Micaiah. But he never says anything good about me. I don't want to listen to him.'

It's tough, isn't it, to be really honest with people – especially when they ask for our advice and we know they aren't going to like the answer? Simply put, we don't want to offend people. We don't want to hurt their feelings.

I am especially grateful for friends who tell me the truth in love. I know they care about me and I can trust their opinion. I believe their advice isn't coming from a skewed perspective or an ulterior motive. I trust them to hear from Jesus, and to remind me of his word and his ways.

There are some awesome, courageous prophets in the Old Testament, but this snapshot of Micaiah is very revealing. At first, he says what the king wants to hear (v. 15). The king doesn't believe him; he knows Micaiah is being sarcastic. So Micaiah then tells him the truth (v. 17). 'There you go,' says Ahab to Jehoshaphat. 'Nothing good. Told you so!'

It's also very revealing that Jehoshaphat knew Ahab wasn't hearing the truth. He insisted he listened to God before deciding on the next step. That's what a great friend does – someone who may not always say what you want them to say, but has your best interests at heart.

Do you have good friends you can trust to remind you of God's ways? Are you a wise counsellor? Reflect on this and bring any thoughts to the Lord.

SHEILA JACOBS

Dangerous alliances

Ahab king of Israel asked Jehoshaphat king of Judah, 'Will you go with me against Ramoth Gilead?' Jehoshaphat replied, 'I am as you are, and my people as your people; we will join you in the war.' (NIV)

It really is worth spending another day learning a lesson from the life of Jehoshaphat. Although he encouraged Ahab to listen to the right counsel, he made a serious error here.

Unlike Jehoshaphat, Ahab was not a good king. But having been asked a favour by Ahab, Jehoshaphat agrees immediately to help him; it seems he sought good relations with the northern tribes (v. 1). As we saw in yesterday's note, the outcome of the battle was not going to be good, but Jehoshaphat goes ahead with the agreement. What a shame he doesn't seek the Lord before consenting to this alliance!

Ahab puts him in danger right from the outset. How? By suggesting Jehoshaphat wear his kingly robes in the battle while Ahab disguises himself. In other words, Jehoshaphat is to be the target! Why the king of Judah agrees to this is anyone's guess. Is he afraid of upsetting Ahab? He compromises himself by this ungodly alliance and soon finds himself in trouble. But he cries out to God and the Lord rescues him. However, he is rebuked by a prophet on his return to Jerusalem (2 Chronicles 19:1–3).

In this whole episode, we can see how dangerous it can be to make alliances with those who do not serve God. We always need to pray before making any big decisions – marriage, career and even close friendships. The Bible warns us about being 'yoked' with unbelievers (2 Corinthians 6:14). Will we be compromised?

While we can be sure that, if we make wrong decisions, God will forgive us if we sincerely repent and cry out to him, let's be careful in our choices. Better to say 'no' than to put ourselves in danger.

Is there compromise in your life? How is it affecting your Christian walk? Bring your concerns to God now and ask him to forgive you (if appropriate), and to counsel and guide you.

SHEILA JACOBS

Your faith or mine?

Joash did what was right in the eyes of the Lord all the years of Jehoiada the priest… After the death of Jehoiada, the officials of Judah came… and he listened to them. They abandoned the temple of the Lord… and worshipped… idols. (NIV)

Young Joash, saved from certain death by his aunt, the wife of the priest Jehoiada, starts so well. But this king finishes badly.

Joash's murderous grandmother was destroying members of the house of Judah. But Joash was miraculously saved and then became king at the tender age of seven, when his grandmother was ousted from power. Jehoiada was behind this coup, and it was really down to this incredible priest that the rightful king, Joash, was placed upon the throne. It is interesting that it is Jehoiada who made the covenant that the new king and his people would be the Lord's (2 Chronicles 23:16). As you read about this king, it is clear that the priest remained the strongest influence in Joash's life.

But what happens after Jehoiada died? It appears that Joash turned right away from the Lord. So we have to conclude that Jehoiada's powerful faith probably wasn't shared by Joash. This king who had repaired the temple seems to have fallen apart spiritually when his faith mentor passed away.

We could, perhaps, surmise that he had been led from an early age rather than growing in his faith independently. Perhaps when the influence departed, and he was left to his own devices, the sudden freedom unbalanced him. But if we are left wondering just where Joash really stood with the Lord, his actions speak volumes.

God has no grandchildren. We don't become Christians because our parents or our grandparents were believers. We have to come to him personally, individually. We can't rely on someone else's faith. Examine yourself – are you relying on someone else's experience of God today, or your own?

Do you have your own personal friendship with Jesus? Do you feel you follow 'from afar'? Ask him to bring you closer.

SHEILA JACOBS

Pride and gratitude

But after Uzziah became powerful, his pride led to his downfall. He was unfaithful to the Lord his God… he was raging at the priests. (NIV)

Uzziah was only 16 when he became king. This passage tells us that he accepted instruction and that, for as long as he sought after God, the Lord granted him success. But success apparently went to his head. The Bible tells us he was 'unfaithful' to God and it appears he takes it upon himself to perform a ritual that is for the priests alone to do – those who are consecrated. When challenged, Uzziah becomes angry. He also becomes ill.

Isn't it interesting to see the change in someone who started so well? But how very easy it is to veer off a straight course and end up somewhere we don't want to be. Pride is insidious. It was Lucifer's sin (Isaiah 14:12–15). It's the sin of 'I will' – me, myself and I. But as Christians, we must never forget to whom we owe everything – even our very breath.

After being in a position of utter helplessness and receiving restoration from God, it's easy to start relying on ourselves once again – or even believing that what we have accomplished, we have done through our own skills and devices. That can lead to pride. But at each meal and each time we can pay a bill, receive a payment, view a perfect sunset or spend time with someone we love, we should thank God.

In the first novel I had published, I quoted this verse: 'All that we have accomplished you have done for us' (Isaiah 26:12). Why? Because before I had that book accepted, I had failed a writing course and my life was shattered by illness. I knew God had opened that door. Perhaps you, like me, need to keep remembering that all we have comes from God's gracious hands.

Pause for a moment and think of three things you can thank God for right now. Do you need to say sorry to God for a prideful attitude?

SHEILA JACOBS

Hold on

In his time of trouble King Ahaz became even more unfaithful to the Lord. He offered sacrifices to the gods… for he thought, 'Since the gods of the kings of Aram have helped them… they will help me.' But they were his downfall. (NIV)

It's worth reading this whole chapter (and perhaps 2 Kings 16 as well, if you have time) just to get a real feel for the complete mess that was Ahaz's life. It strikes me how sad it is. People follow a leader – and what a poor example of leadership Ahaz was.

He has already committed acts of real atrocity (v. 3). Here, we watch him slide further and further away from God.

Often in a crisis any veneer drops away, and we see what we really believe. What do we do when we're desperate? Where do we go?

People who don't know Jesus can get into a real pickle, trying all sorts of alternative spiritual realities. This way leads only to deeper darkness, as they wander further away from the light. Maybe this was you before you called out to Jesus. Or perhaps you have friends or family who are trying spiritual alternatives, rather than choosing to come to him. Perhaps someone you know is in crisis and thinking, 'I've prayed; it doesn't work. God doesn't exist. I'll try something else.' Or maybe this is your current experience.

If it is, I urge you to not give up on the one who loves you and can change people and circumstances. Trust him. Don't turn away from him. We are fully dependent on him for rescue and release. In fact, as I hope you are beginning to see through these notes, we are always dependent on God; it's just that sometimes we aren't so aware of it. God in his kindness may use points of crisis to show us where our faith is really at. Hold on to him – and his promises (see Isaiah 43:1–2).

If you know anyone who is struggling in their faith, pray for them now. If it's you, ask God to show you some of his promises. Believe him!

SHEILA JACOBS

Getting serious

'Now, Lord our God, deliver us from [the king of Assyria's] hand, so that all the kingdoms of the earth may know that you alone, Lord, are God.' (NIV)

There are two things in Hezekiah's story that really strike me, so let's look at the first one today and the second one tomorrow.

Hezekiah, having purified the temple and celebrated Passover, is threatened by a mocking assailant, the king of Assyria, who tries to undermine the people's faith in their king and their God (2 Kings 18:28–35). Hezekiah, having failed to negotiate terms with Assyria, goes to the Lord in the temple. His enemy, Sennacherib, is laying siege to Judah's fortified cities. Hezekiah needs help.

I like the way he spreads out his problem before the Lord (v. 14). This is serious prayer. He appeals to God to show his hand for his own glory. And following on, we see that his prayer was heard (see 19:20–34).

Does it take a crisis for you to really seek God's face? In 2016, I had a serious health scare. People were very kind and said things like 'Trust God', 'You're healed, just believe' or 'Don't worry – even if it's the worst-case scenario, the doctors can work wonders.' But I knew I had to get a hold of Jesus for myself. Then, one night, he spoke to me, saying, 'Nothing the enemy can do will stop my plan for your life.' At that point, I knew everything would be okay. And, praise God, it was.

There are times when nothing less than this kind of diligent prayer will do. 'Okay, God, I'm in crisis. I need to hear from you…' Crying, being real, then waiting, listening, trusting.

Do you need to get serious in prayer today, for yourself or someone else?

Use your own words to get real with God about any situation that is weighing heavily on you. Ask him for the words and ask him for the answers. Then ask him for peace, and wait.

SHEILA JACOBS

A temporary home

'This is what the Lord, the God of your father David, says: I have heard your prayer and seen your tears; I will heal you.' (NIV)

King Hezekiah is ill to 'the point of death'. Isaiah the prophet tells him that the Lord has said he won't recover. He must 'put [his] house in order' (v. 1) – something that perhaps we all need to think about, even if we are fit and well.

Hezekiah prays and weeps. And God is merciful, adding 15 years to his life – promising to deliver the city from its enemies, too. I love the sign that is given to Hezekiah: the shadow going backwards up the steps.

We see here the compassion of God – and that he is a God of miracles, including healing. We may wonder why some are healed and some are not. But these bodies aren't made to live on this earth forever. Human beings are made in the image of God, as Genesis tells us, but it's when we believe and receive Jesus, our Saviour, that we are given 'the right to become children of God' (John 1:12). It is sobering to remember that our lives on earth, even if we are blessed with many years, are actually very brief – and choices we make here will affect eternity.

I remember looking at a rose-covered jug and bowl I'd bought. I loved it, but I thought, 'One day, it'll belong to someone else.' We're only stewards of our possessions – be it houses, clothes, trinkets, whatever. And we are stewards, too, of our bodies; we need to treat them well. But this world is our temporary home.

Let's remember to hold lightly everything that we have. If we know Jesus, we are 'aliens and strangers' on earth (1 Peter 2:11, NIV 1984). Jesus is preparing a place for us (John 14:1–4). And one day, he'll take us to be where he is.

If you know Jesus, give thanks to God for the unseen eternal home that you are part of. If you don't know him, ask him to reveal himself to you today.

SHEILA JACOBS

A new understanding

'Because your heart was responsive and you humbled yourself before God when you heard what he spoke against this place and its people, and because you humbled yourself before me and tore your robes and wept in my presence, I have heard you, declares the Lord.' (NIV)

The next king we're looking at, Josiah, appears to have been devoted to the Lord from an early age. In his 20s, he begins repairing the temple, which obviously has been neglected. But then something happens. The Book of the Law is discovered. Part of it is read to the king. And when he hears it, he tears his robes, a sign of great anguish and grief as he realises how far his people have strayed from the Lord.

The prophet Huldah is consulted, and God gives a warning of future destruction. God says, however, that he has seen Josiah's humility and for that reason will be gracious to him personally. God's grace – his patience, love and forgiveness – never cease to amaze me.

True repentance means a change of heart, a changing of the ways. The prodigal son in Jesus' story (found in Luke 15) was repentant. Humbled, he realised how wrong he had been. He also did something about it: he came home.

Josiah's shock is evident as he gains a new understanding of God's will and requirements. The way to know what God requires of us is to read his word. We need to know what's in it in order to live by it, by the power of the Spirit. It is divine counsel, and we need to trust it more than we trust our own feelings and ideas. Sometimes, we think we know what God requires – but have we checked with the Bible? And will we make consequent decisions based on God's word?

Reading a little ahead, verse 33 says that the people followed the Lord as long as Josiah was alive. We need strong leaders with godly vision and biblical authority in our fellowships and in our society – those who will make a stand for God's word and encourage others to do so!

Do you need a fresh understanding of God's word? Why not ask him for a new desire to read it, to know his will and to follow him more closely?

SHEILA JACOBS

Critical attitude

Josiah, however, would not turn away from [Necho king of Egypt], but disguised himself to engage him in battle. He would not listen to what Necho had said at God's command but went to fight him on the plain of Megiddo. (NIV)

Josiah reads the Book of the Law to the people and renews the covenant, making the people 'pledge themselves to it' (2 Chronicles 34:30–32). He removes idols and spiritists, purging the land with great fervency (2 Kings 23:4–16, 24). He also puts the ark back in the temple (interesting that it appears to have been removed) and celebrates the Passover. 2 Kings 23:22 implies that the Passover hadn't been kept in a very long time.

So reforms were made; it wasn't just about repairing the temple – it was about following God. We're told that never was there a king like Josiah, 'who turned to the Lord as he did – with all his heart… soul and… strength' (2 Kings 23:25). But then he makes a spectacular error of judgement.

The king of Egypt was ready for war – but not, apparently, with Judah. Yet Josiah goes out to fight him anyway. King Necho issues a warning, saying that Josiah is opposing God by coming to fight. Josiah refuses to 'listen to what Necho had said at God's command' (v. 22) – and it costs him his life. Was it arrogance? Did he not believe that God could speak through the Egyptian? If he had sought the Lord at this point, he would have surely not gone to war. What a tragic end for someone who clearly loved and served God.

Sometimes God may choose someone to warn us, rebuke us or give us wise counsel. But we don't want to hear it. Why? Because of who is advising us! However, just because we may not acknowledge their credentials, always agree with them or even like them, that doesn't mean God can't use them. Sometimes we have to put our own feelings in a box and learn to be objective.

Lord, when you use someone I don't particularly like or admire to speak your words, help me to receive them. Forgive me for judging, and for any critical attitude I may hold.

SHEILA JACOBS

The king's table

[The king of Babylon] spoke kindly to [Jehoiachin] and gave him a seat of honour higher than those of the other kings who were with him in Babylon. So Jehoiachin put aside his prison clothes and for the rest of his life ate regularly at the king's table. (NIV)

The last ruler of Judah I want us to look at is King Jehoiachin. The Bible tells us that 'he did evil in the eyes of the Lord, just as his father had done' (24:9). During his reign, King Nebuchadnezzar of Babylon laid siege to Jerusalem, and Jehoiachin and all his officials surrendered to him. The temple was plundered and Jehoiachin taken captive. Jehoiachin's uncle, Zedekiah, was made a puppet king in his place. Then Zedekiah rebelled and, under siege again, Jerusalem finally fell to the power of Babylon.

2 Kings 24:20 says: 'It was because of the Lord's anger that all this happened to Jerusalem and Judah, and in the end he thrust them from his presence.' Zedekiah was clearly not a godly king, but he wasn't the only one. We saw right at the start of this series that God is a covenant God. His people had consistently turned away from his loving kindness.

Judah had good kings and bad kings: those who sought to lead the people in God's ways – and those who did not.

So why do I want to end with Jehoiachin? Well, it seems that a new king of Babylon had mercy on him. He set him free from his prison and restored honour to him. Perhaps Jehoiachin had been praying for mercy during his long captivity. Or maybe not. Perhaps the king was simply benevolent and compassionate, speaking 'kindly' to a man who couldn't free himself and who did not deserve the grace lavished upon him.

I'm sure you can see the parallel. We are prisoners to sin and darkness whom a kind and gracious king is willing to set free. We can 'put aside [our] prison clothes' and eat at the king's table, our dignity restored. What a wonderful offer.

Do you need to be set free from prison clothes? Jesus offers you a place at his table. Come to him now, and receive his life, his love and his presence.

SHEILA JACOBS

The church is born:
Acts 1—12

Claire Musters writes:

The New Testament starts with four accounts of the person and work of Jesus Christ. Acts is the very next book – and it is full of history as well as encouragement to us that we, too, can do the miracles that Jesus did and continue to spread the gospel. Acts was written by Luke, and we can see the similarities between it and his gospel. He finished that gospel by telling us that Jesus was taken up into heaven, and Acts is the next instalment. While Luke's gospel concentrates on who Jesus was and what he did while on earth, Acts reveals what he has done since ascending to heaven.

Acts starts by repeating some of the information covered at the end of Luke, but then moves on to give an accurate historical account of the lives of the early Christians.

However, Acts is much more than history – it is also a theological look at the Holy Spirit's early work in God's people. It is incredible to see the same group of disciples who had run scared at Jesus' arrest, now empowered and spreading the gospel – fulfilling the commission that he had given them while on earth. It is such an encouragement to reflect that they really had nothing going for them, except that God had chosen them – and that is all they needed. How amazing that he chooses us today!

In the first twelve chapters of Acts, we see the Holy Spirit fall like fire, the disciples persecuted and the beginnings of church growth. Reading through, we witness the birth of the global church that we are a part of, and the unity and care that the early Christians showed one another can be a real challenge to us.

They also experienced some birthing and growing pains. The lessons learned about what constitutes a healthy church can be helpful for us today.

Peter is a central character in this first part of Acts. Speaking to the crowds – and authorities – on various occasions, he was also the one that God spoke to about the all-encompassing work of Jesus: the gospel was and is available to all. Let us celebrate and remember that – as well as being open to what God wants to teach us as we delve into Acts together.

Chosen and commissioned

'You will receive power when the Holy Spirit comes on you; and you will be my witnesses in Jerusalem, and in all Judea and Samaria, and to the ends of the earth.' (NIV)

Luke begins his book by addressing Theophilus, the same person he wrote to in his gospel. Meaning 'friend of God', Theophilus may have been someone's name, such as a Roman acquaintance interested in Christianity, a patron or the judge for Paul's trial, or it may have been a general term for all believers. Whoever it was, Luke reminds the reader that his first book was dedicated to all Jesus did and said. He repeats the instructions that Jesus gave the disciples (also recorded in Luke 24:49): 'Do not leave Jerusalem, but wait for the gift my Father promised' (v. 4). Jesus knew that it was this power from on high that would enable them to fulfil the commission he had given them in Matthew 28:19: 'Go and make disciples of all nations, baptising them in the name of the Father and of the Son and of the Holy Spirit.'

Without the Holy Spirit's empowering, we likewise can do nothing. Waiting on him in prayer is so important, and it is interesting to see that that is exactly what the believers did while they waited for him to come. Running ahead in our own strength is not helpful. Remaining in him, and accepting his timing, is a sign of maturity (note that the disciples did this together).

A replacement for Judas is chosen too – under the direction of God through prayer and the casting of lots. This was a common practice in those times.

In verse 15, we see a glimpse of 'the Rock' stepping into the role Jesus had for him. Having changed his name from Simon to Peter (Matthew 16:17–18), Jesus later commissioned him to feed his church (John 21:15–19). We will see how he became the first big champion of the gospel after the Holy Spirit came, speaking fearlessly in front of crowds of people.

Ask God to help you remain constantly aware of his presence today, to wait patiently as necessary, but also to speak up when prompted.

CLAIRE MUSTERS

Fire falls

All of them were filled with the Holy Spirit and began to speak in other tongues as the Spirit enabled them. (NIV)

On the day of Pentecost, the apostles and other believers were still gathered, waiting for the promised Holy Spirit. What happened was a dramatic, sudden outpouring, which marked the birth of the church.

The word 'Spirit' is translated from the Greek *pneuma*, which means breath or breeze, so it is appropriate that the Holy Spirit's coming is described as being like 'the blowing of a violent wind' (v. 2). There are many instances of the image of wind being used to describe God's hand at work, such as in Ezekiel 37, where God breathes life into dead bones.

The description also includes tongues of fire – in fulfilment of John the Baptist's prophecy (Luke 3:16) – while the outpouring itself reflects Joel's prophecy (Joel 2:28–29). The image of fire being associated with God's presence occurs elsewhere, such as when Moses heard God speak to him through the burning bush (Exodus 3) and the fire on Mount Sinai (Exodus 19). God also miraculously burnt up the offerings on Mount Carmel to show his power and presence (1 Kings 18). The imagery here reflects the fact that Pentecost was a divine act of God, fulfilling his will and purpose: preparing them to be his witnesses.

Just as some onlookers thought the believers had had too much wine, people can believe that we, today, are strange for seeking to live our lives under the direction of the Holy Spirit. But it is their vision that is blinkered. In Acts, those who were mocking didn't ponder the fact that they were each hearing the believers talking in their own language. That is such a miracle; rather than a drunken mess, there was beautiful order to the way the Holy Spirit fell.

Do you see this kind of mixed response among your friends and family? Does it ever get you down? Pray for grace and strength from the Holy Spirit in order to respond well.

CLAIRE MUSTERS

The evangelist steps forward

'Repent and be baptised, every one of you, in the name of Jesus Christ for the forgiveness of your sins. And you will receive the gift of the Holy Spirit.' (NIV)

This is the first of Peter's major speeches, in which he bore witness to all he knew about Jesus – and the Holy Spirit.

Peter started by directly addressing the murmurings of the crowd, quoting the passage in Joel (Joel 2:28–29) to show that what was happening had been prophesied.

From verse 22, Peter spoke clearly about who Jesus was – and is, following his resurrection. He proclaimed powerfully, 'God has raised this Jesus to life, and we are all witnesses of it' (v. 32). Peter's impassioned speech was a far cry from his earlier behaviour of denying Jesus.

We can take comfort from the fact that even our most shameful secrets do not negate God's calling. Just as my husband and I were helping to start a church, very painful circumstances caused me to make a foolish decision. As a result, we stepped back for a while, but, as we wrestled with whether we should stay, God spoke to us about the fact that he had never asked us to leave. (Details are in my book *Taking Off the Mask*.)

The crowd responded to the newly restored and emboldened Peter with 'What shall we do?' (v. 37). He wanted to ensure that conversion was genuine so was very clear about the need for repentance and baptism. The first is a recognition of sin, and a turning away from it while asking for forgiveness. Baptism was historically for Gentiles who had turned to Judaism, so this was a hard thing for Jews to do. But it would reveal their hearts – and join them with other believers. As well as instructing them, Peter promised they would receive the Holy Spirit. God's heart is to bless us; even though being his disciples is costly, what he lavishes on us is worth far more!

Lord, I am struck by how clear Peter's speech was, empowered by the Holy Spirit: he was not afraid to speak up. Help me not to shy away from opportunities to share my faith when you present them to me.

CLAIRE MUSTERS

Template for the church

They devoted themselves to the apostles' teaching and to fellowship, to the breaking of bread and to prayer. (NIV)

Our reading for today is much shorter than others, but packs a punch! It is a summary of what being a disciple is about – and how to keep a church healthy.

Just ponder: in verse 41 we were told that there were 3,000 converts on the day of Pentecost, and only 120 had been waiting in that upper room when the Holy Spirit descended (see Acts 1:15). So how did such a small number disciple so many?

The description we see in this end part of Acts 2 reveals that they followed Jesus' model. He had told them to leave everything and follow him (see, for example, Matthew 4:19–20). In our passage, we see that there were both large meetings in the temple and smaller ones in people's homes. Everyone was devoted to 'doing life' together: they followed the teaching they received, spent time together, broke bread to remember Jesus' sacrifice, prayed regularly and, by sharing all they had, ensured that no one among them was in need. And we are told that they had 'glad and sincere hearts' (v. 46).

This passage is full of challenges and encouragements. How often does the individualism of our culture rub off on us, causing us to look at how church can fulfil *our* needs rather than thinking about how we can give of ourselves to help those around us?

I know that, in our busy lives, it is easy to squeeze church into a few spare hours on a Sunday morning, and perhaps a midweek meeting. While that superficially looks like the format for church described here, the spirit behind these verses could too easily be lost. Being devoted to one another and to God takes time.

While this passage is a great template for church life, I know that it can seem like a tall order in our time-starved society. However, God can give us creative ways to 'do life' together. Ask for his ideas today.

CLAIRE MUSTERS

Reflecting Jesus

Peter looked straight at [the lame man], as did John. Then Peter said, 'Look at us!' (NIV)

Yesterday, we looked at the close fellowship within the early church, and in the first verse of Acts 3 we see that Peter and John were going to the temple *together*. Peter was not a lone ranger; even with his gift of eloquent, bold speaking (which he employs again later in the chapter), he still ministered alongside others. This is a great reminder to us that we are called to work alongside others, rather than on our own. We are told in 1 Corinthians 12:12–31 that we are part of a body that will not function properly if we do not all play our part – and allow others to play theirs. John and Peter were very different characters, but still worked alongside one another.

The lame man they met at the temple gate had been disabled from birth, which would have meant disgrace and poverty. He had positioned himself at the gate Beautiful to beg for money – but he got so much more when Peter and John stopped to speak to him. They looked straight at him, giving him dignity, and then told him to look at them. Yet again, they were bearing witness to who Jesus was (and Peter goes on in verses 11–26 to give a similar speech to the one we've already looked at). But this time, they were doing so through reflecting Jesus: by looking at them, the man was seeing his Saviour. Filled with the same Spirit, Peter was able to give the man his health back – something far more precious than money. This revealed Jesus not only to the man, but to all those around them. He may have been positioned at the gate Beautiful, but the disciples showed him, and those watching and listening, someone far more beautiful.

The beauty of faith can captivate hearts. This miracle gave an opportunity for sharing the gospel; why not pray for miracles and opportunities in your neighbourhood?

CLAIRE MUSTERS

Persecution begins

When they saw the courage of Peter and John and realised that they were unschooled, ordinary men, they were astonished and they took note that these men had been with Jesus. (NIV)

It is no coincidence that, just after reading about a miracle, today we read about Peter and John being thrown into jail. Their message 'greatly disturbed' (v. 2) the Sadducees. Yet they could not deny the impact of what Peter and John were doing and saying: in verse 4, we are told that 5,000 believed. Peter and John were taken before the Jewish council, who wanted to know: 'By what power or what name did you do this?' (v. 7).

Again, we see the effect of the Holy Spirit on Peter: he is able to speak clearly and eloquently about Jesus and deliver the gospel message to them.

The leaders could not deny what had happened, but they did try to suppress people talking about it (v. 18). This can happen to us too: we can feel intimidated by others' reaction to our faith – but the name of Jesus is just as powerful today and we need to look to him rather than to them (see vv. 19–20).

Once released, Peter and John didn't hide away; they immediately went to their friends. What was the whole group's response to their growing concern about Peter and John's safety? Prayer. God responded by sending more of his Spirit upon them and they began to speak boldly.

I find their response so challenging; I'm not sure prayer is the first response I have when I face difficulties – and in particular, ridicule or harsh treatment from others. Their response to 'threats' was to ask for the ability to 'speak your word with great boldness' (v. 29). I long to be as affected by the name of Jesus daily as they so obviously were. What about you?

Lord, I long to be as full of faith as those I've read about today. I cannot do it in my own strength. Please fill me afresh with your Spirit so that I will share you wherever I go today.

CLAIRE MUSTERS

Hearts revealed

'What made you think of doing such a thing? You have not lied just to human beings but to God.' (NIV)

Acts 5 starts by describing a couple who, like Joseph Barnabas in the previous chapter (see 4:36–37), sold something they owned, then took the money to the apostles. The difference between the two instances is that Ananias and Sapphira lied in order to hold some of the money back. It wasn't the withholding itself that was wrong, but rather the lying about it (vv. 3–4). To our modern eyes, it seems harsh for God to strike them down, but their actions revealed the state of their hearts. What they were doing was divisive and potentially fatal for the church, which was built on generosity and openness – as well as genuine witness to Jesus. While on the outside they may have seemed virtuous, inside they were ruled by a love of money. It is sobering to take stock of why we do what we do within church – and elsewhere. Is it to look good, or is it being done as an act of worship before God, regardless of what recognition we get from others?

The state of the Sadducees' hearts is revealed from verse 17 onwards. Again, the apostles were doing miracles and more people believed, and we read that 'the high priest and all his associates… were filled with jealousy' (v. 17). It was this that fuelled their decision to arrest the apostles again. God's response was miraculously to open the jail doors. When confronted for speaking out again, the apostles' hearts were revealed: 'We must obey God rather than human beings!' (v. 29). With such a message and personal witness, they could not help but do as God asked.

Do we regularly take the time to dwell on what God has done for us? When we do, gratitude and a willingness to obey are the natural response.

Take some time today before God and ask him to examine your heart, as David did at the end of Psalm 139. Ask him to reveal areas that need work, and submit to his lordship afresh.

CLAIRE MUSTERS

Stephen: a shining example

All who were sitting in the Sanhedrin looked intently at Stephen, and they saw that his face was like the face of an angel. (NIV)

The start of Acts 6 is refreshing, as it shows there were teething problems in the early church – things weren't perfect, even then. With growth came challenges but, rather than ignoring them, the leaders met them head-on and provided a solution: delegation. When a church is functioning well, each person will have the opportunity to use their gifts to serve others. Here, seven men were chosen to meet the specific need – and one is singled out in the rest of Acts 6—7. Stephen was known for being full of grace, wisdom and power; the religious leaders didn't like that! In response, verse 13 says they 'produced false witnesses'.

Has that ever happened to you? How have you responded when people have falsely accused you? It doesn't tell us how Stephen acted, but we see how serene he looked.

It is worth reading his lengthy speech (7:2–53), which is the longest in the book of Acts. While it was he who had been put on trial for blasphemy, Stephen's eloquent response puts the Sanhedrin on trial – although they did not recognise it; rather, they dragged him out and stoned him. His response in court and when set upon reminds me of Jesus' – he too was calm and steadfast, but also asked the Father to forgive his accusers, as Stephen does while being stoned (7:60).

Stephen's stoning was the start of the church's persecution – as believers mourned him, they also scattered, which was the way the church spread (see 8:1–2).

We may never face physical persecution, but there will be those who disregard our witness and/or reject us. We can, however, learn to find our security in God rather than others, in order to stand firm and be shining examples like Stephen.

Lord, Stephen's story is hugely challenging and inspiring. Help me to look always to you, and to remain faithful even when others mock or reject me.

CLAIRE MUSTERS

Teaching with clarity

The Spirit told Philip, 'Go to that chariot and stay near it.' (NIV)

In today's reading, we see two instances of the growing church reaching those around who were open to the gospel. In those days, there were many sorcerers and magicians. But something had gripped Simon's heart; he saw that the miracles Philip was doing were due to a higher power. Even after believing and being baptised, he still equated such 'magical' powers with money, and tried to buy the ability to empower others with the Holy Spirit. Peter, in his usual forthright style, challenged him (vv. 20–23).

While I would not advocate Peter's style here, I do think it is important that we carefully and graciously correct mistaken beliefs new Christians may have. As our society becomes less and less based on Christianity, there is a growing number of people who have little idea of the teachings of our faith; we mustn't assume knowledge and then sit in judgement over them.

I love reading this second story, which shows how clearly Philip heard from God. The resulting encounter led an Ethiopian official to embrace the good news and be baptised. We can learn from Philip's approach: he took his cues from where the man already was (he was reading Isaiah) and offered to explain. Doing this enables us to share the gospel with grace.

I love it when the Holy Spirit leads us so specifically. I recently spoke at a church and took a friend with me. She heard from God and was able to share an encouraging word with someone – God had even told her his name! God loves to be directly involved as we go about ministering to others in life. How often do you ask him for his input in your day?

Lord, please help me not to judge those around me. Also help me to keep my spiritual eyes and ears open to the opportunities you may be putting in front of me to share my faith today.

CLAIRE MUSTERS

Saul's conversion and commissioning

'I am Jesus, whom you are persecuting,' he replied. 'Now get up and go into the city, and you will be told what you must do.' (NIV)

The first time we came across Saul, he was looking after the coats of those stoning Stephen, and he went on to spend all his energy persecuting the church. In Acts 9, however, God catches up with him! Even today, people use the term 'Damascus Road experience' to describe a dramatic conversion story; we get to read the original here!

When I read this account, I am struck by how obedient – and brave – Ananias was. He may have been tempted to question God's instruction that he visit Saul the murderer of Christians (v. 13), but then he simply accepted that God had a calling on Saul's life.

As soon as Saul received his sight, he started preaching the gospel. His presentation would have been all the more arresting as people remembered how he used to persecute the church.

There's a lesson for us here: how often do we imply to new believers that they need to wait until they are more mature to do things for God? It is up to God to decide when and how to use each one of us. While it is important for the mature to instruct the less mature, we must be careful not to hold people back.

I love the fact that Barnabas appears again here. We first read of him in 4:36–37 selling a field and giving money to the apostles; here, we learn that he supported Saul when he tried to join the disciples in Jerusalem. Understandably, they were scared of Saul, but Barnabas bore witness to his changed life. He went against the opinion held within the rest of the group, even though he was probably scared too. There may be times when God calls us to do something like that. Are we willing to?

Ananias was an ordinary, faithful Christian, yet God made him instrumental in the conversion of a man who was to write so much of the New Testament. Just think how God may use you!

CLAIRE MUSTERS

God's good news for all

'Do not call anything impure that God has made clean.' (NIV)

At the end of Acts 9, Peter raises someone from the dead, but even though he was so full of God's Spirit, he still needed some theological training by God – which is what happens here. I find that challenging and it reminds me that, even though I have been a Christian for many years, hold leadership positions in my church and speak elsewhere regularly, I still have new things to learn of God and from God.

What Peter learned here made a huge difference to the history of the church. He assumed that he had a right view of the Gentiles; God showed him he was wrong! And God was very graphic in the way that he provided the lesson. I think it reveals not only the gravity of the lesson, but also God's amazing creativity and how far he was prepared to go to show Peter that his love extends to everyone. How incredible to be put into a trance, to see such an extraordinary sight and then to hear the voice of God. And yet Peter still felt the need to be 'righteous' under the old law and keep himself 'clean'.

God prepared Cornelius' heart for the truth, too. I love God's attention to detail. Cornelius was a centurion in the Roman army – someone the disciples would have seen as an enemy more than a brother. But when God speaks, we need to take note, as he could be challenging a long-held wrong belief. If Peter hadn't eventually accepted God's lesson, we might not have heard the good news for ourselves – now that's a sobering thought! Could it be that there are people who seem to you to be 'beyond' the gospel? Why not take the time to pray for them today?

Lord, I am so grateful that you challenged Peter's beliefs in order to open the gospel up fully to the Gentiles. Help me to heed your teaching closely as I go about my day.

CLAIRE MUSTERS

Peter defends his actions

When Peter went up to Jerusalem, the circumcised believers criticised him. (NIV)

Yesterday, we saw how God showed Peter that he must not call anything impure that God has deemed pure (10:15). Once at Cornelius' house, Peter began to teach the good news to those gathered, but, while speaking, he must have had questions going through his mind: should I lead them to Christ? Should I baptise them? What will this mean for the church if I do? And yet again, God steps in with the final word: the Holy Spirit fell 'on all who heard the message' (10:44). Suddenly, those who had accompanied Peter had their theology blown too! And, once Peter saw it, he realised he must baptise all those who believe.

Even though God had moved in such an amazing way, Peter was criticised by other believers (11:2). Isn't that often the way? While we may expect a backlash from those outside the church, sometimes the criticism comes from within – which can make it all the more painful. And the criticism can be petty, too: 'You went into the house of uncircumcised men and ate with them' (v. 3). Okay, to the Jews he had broken God's commandments laid out in the Old Testament – but shouldn't hearing about the number who had come to faith have affected their viewpoint? And shouldn't there have been some rejoicing going on?

Have you ever experienced God working through you, only to have another Christian complain about it? I know that to be extremely painful, but we can learn from what Peter did here. He took time to explain exactly what God had said to him and why he had done what he did. By graciously answering their misgivings, he enabled them eventually to praise God. Meeting opposition, from whatever quarter, with grace and love is a great way of disarming it.

God, when I am criticised by those with whom I am united in Christ, as I surely will be, help me to respond with grace as Peter did, rather than becoming immobilised through sadness or anger.

CLAIRE MUSTERS

Faithfulness as the church spreads

For a whole year Barnabas and Saul met with the church and taught great numbers of people. (NIV)

Today, we see the impact of the persecution following Stephen's martyrdom: as people scattered, the gospel was spread far and wide. In Antioch, the believers made a particular effort to spread the good news to Gentiles. While those in Jerusalem had accepted Peter's explanation, perhaps they became alarmed when they were hit with the reality of many Gentiles becoming Christians. Whatever their reason, they sent Barnabas to investigate. True to his name and nature, he was encouraged by what he saw and spent time investing in the church. Taking Saul, too, he stayed for a whole year.

I find this challenging, particularly as these chapters are all about the spread of the early church. While many of the teachers travelled from church to church, Barnabas and Saul stayed put for a considerable period. Do we sometimes want to move on to the next exciting thing, while God is asking us to be faithful where we are? It was vital that the new believers were discipled well. Do we take the time to do that in our churches?

I also find it intriguing to read about Agabus in verse 28. Having travelled himself from Jerusalem, he prophesied about a famine that occurred during the reign of Emperor Claudius. It is so wonderful to read how the church in Antioch responded: by giving all that they could to help others.

This passage is about individuals faithfully doing what God had asked them to do. 1 Corinthians 12:12–31 tells us that we are part of one body, and each one of us has a vital part to play. Reading about Barnabas the encourager, Barnabas and Saul the teachers and Agabus the prophet, as well as the generosity of the believers in Antioch, shows us that this was a church that knew how to be 'the body of Christ'.

Lord, help me to learn from the church and leaders I have read about in Antioch, and to be faithful in doing what you have asked of me.

CLAIRE MUSTERS

Peter's miraculous escape

'You're out of your mind,' they told her. When she kept insisting that it was so, they said, 'It must be his angel.' (NIV)

We end our look at the first twelve chapters of Acts with an incredible story of rescue. Peter has featured in much of what we have discussed, and is the main character here too.

This passage immediately reminded me that God doesn't always stop us from experiencing difficulties. Here, we read that James had already been put to death and that Herod went on to seize Peter, presumably with the same intention. We might think that God should have protected them, but Jesus warned us that believing in him would not shield us from trouble (John 16:33). However, we can still trust him. What we may find difficult is that he doesn't always do things as we expect. While this passage shows a dramatic rescue of Peter, what about James? Why was he not rescued? I don't believe we will get answers to such questions until we reach heaven, when we will look back with God's whole perspective, rather than our very limited one.

One thing that does strike me is how the church was 'earnestly praying to God' (v. 5). I am not suggesting that they didn't pray for James, but I do believe that when we pray it makes a difference. I find it amusing that when Peter knocks on the door of the very place where they are praying for him, they don't believe it is him and try to come up with another explanation. I wonder if that's how we can be when we pray? Are we so wrapped up in what we are doing that we miss God's answer? And, when it comes, do we try to explain it away rather than simply marvelling at what God has done? I tend to be cynical, so have to guard my heart against that.

Think about what has impacted you positively in the last few weeks, and ask God to embed that in your heart. You may want to ask him to help you pray with faith, and recognise it when he answers.

CLAIRE MUSTERS

Hearing God's voice

Michele D. Morrison writes:

From Genesis to Revelation, we read of a God who speaks.

My husband Don and I have been married for over 40 years. He doesn't always need to speak for me to hear his voice. When an issue arises, I can 'hear' what he would say. His 'voice' is more than an audible vibration; it encompasses the essence of who he is. Recognising God's voice takes time and practice, and grows out of deepening love for him. As we linger in his presence, his voice becomes familiar. The deeper the love, the more profound the communication. God is communicating with us all the time and longs for us to enter into closer relationship with him. If I'm not hearing him, it's not because he isn't talking to me.

We were created for relationship with God, now and forever. Hearing God's voice matters hugely, not just for our own personal edification, though that is an amazing consequence of aligning our hearts, minds and spirits with the thoughts of our creator. Additionally, we seek to hear God's voice in order to be his channel to communicate light and life into a dark and dying world; to be his mouthpiece speaking hope and peace into despairing and anxious hearts; to encourage fellow pilgrims by passing on a prophetic word of love from the Father, who is love. We are drawn closer together as family as we use the supernatural gifts with which we are blessed.

Are you longing for his voice? Are you excited to speak prophetic words into the lives of the weary? Let's get our spiritual antennae up and learn to recognise interference from the world, family and friends, or our own thoughts, so that we can attune ourselves to God's signal.

Don and I listen to BBC Radio 4 in the car, and as we travel, we need to retune the dial because the signal grows weak as we leave one area and enter another. Life is a journey, an adventure in which we need to be alert to God, always fine-tuning our hearts to ensure it is his voice we are hearing and obeying.

Over the next two weeks, we are going to look at some of the ways that God speaks to us. I pray we are all encouraged to listen expectantly with every sensory gift with which we have been blessed.

His sheep know his voice

'The shepherd calls the sheep by name and leads them out. The sheep follow their shepherd, who leads them. The sheep follow the shepherd because they know their shepherd's voice.' (The Source)

My mother grew up on a farm in Wisconsin, USA. As a teenager, she bottle-fed an orphaned lamb. Queenie would follow Mom, unbridled, into the county fair judging ring, where she won prizes. She only responded to Mom's voice.

This parable is so familiar to us; the people sitting with Jesus and listening to his audible voice, however, 'didn't understand what he was telling them' (v. 6). The revelation of the truth of Jesus' identity was probably unexpected and certainly shocking, and they needed clarification. 'Therefore, Jesus said again…' (v. 7). He graciously repeats himself. How often he repeats his truths for us, if only we will listen!

In Jesus' day, a shepherd lived with his sheep and knew each one by name. The sheep were comfortable and confident in his presence. They knew his habits, his voice, his smell. Jesus knows our voices and declares that we, his sheep, know his. He invites, even expects, us to live so close to him that we know his habits, his voice, even his fragrance. How?

Brother Lawrence coined a phrase in the 17th century: 'Practise the presence of God.' Practise. When I set out on a solo car journey, I picture Jesus riding alongside me. I talk to him; I sing to him; I share my heart; and I listen. I practise his presence. It's easy to do when I'm alone. The challenge is to walk through daily life, which can be noisy and demanding, with the same awareness of his presence. In a fold of many sheep bleating noisily, and more than one shepherd, a flock still heard and recognised the voice of their shepherd. They trusted him to protect them from predators, to lead them to green pastures and fresh water, and in his presence they were at peace. Jesus is our peace.

Lord Jesus, may I walk through each day eager to hear your voice, alert to signs of your presence. As I learn your ways, may I sense you moment by moment.

MICHELE D. MORRISON

Hearing and doing

He answered, 'My mother and my brothers are those who hear God's word and do it.' (The Source)

Jesus' disciples ask for clarification of the parable. 'Consider carefully how you listen,' Jesus instructs.

This story links hearing with obedience. God is always speaking – in our hearts, through other people, through the Bible. Some people are spiritually deaf. Others hear God and respond with excitement, but as the thrill wanes, they fall away. Only those whose roots are nourished in the Saviour flourish and bear fruit. They feed on his word and drink the living water of his presence. And who are they? 'My mother and my brothers.'

Mother and brothers. Family. Wow! Jesus came to reconcile us to the Father, enabling us to live close to the Almighty through himself. Gathered under his wings, sheltering in the shadow of the Most High, we hear his voice. When a child cuddles on to her parent's lap and presses her ear into a beloved chest, she hears the voice resonating through the body of the parent rather than from larynx to eardrum. God calls us to himself and he holds us close, so close that our hearts beat in time. We hear the word, retain it and persevere, living a fruitful life.

As a mother and grandmother, I know that often, when I hold a special one close to me, I murmur sweet nothings over them: 'Hello, angel'; 'Jesus loves you'; 'I love you'; 'You are so special.'

When my Bible study group engaged in an exercise together of trying to hear what God is saying, one dear lady, whose struggles in life have resulted in two suicide attempts, heard God declare, 'You are my daughter.' What a 'sweet nothing', a precious confirmation of her identity and her position in his family.

Being family isn't about doing chores. It's about living close. It's about love.

Father God, may I draw near to you, quiet as a weaned child, resting in your love, comforted and at peace as I hear you sing over me with joyful songs.

MICHELE D. MORRISON

Surprised by his voice

Suddenly the Lord called out, 'Samuel!' 'Yes?' Samuel replied. 'What is it?' (NLT)

God called Samuel by name – I love that. It shows that each one of us is special. Samuel initially didn't recognise God's voice. Three times he ran to Eli, and finally Eli realised what was happening and gave him good counsel. Samuel was in the place where he might have expected to hear God, but Eli's own disobedience had built a sound barrier between Samuel and God; perhaps Eli even thought God no longer spoke to his people. His own expectations had died, so probably he hadn't taught Samuel to expect God to speak. Living in disobedience dulls our spiritual ears and kills our expectations.

Even when we are living close to God, though (as Samuel was in the temple), there are times when God's voice penetrates our distracted thoughts, but we don't recognise him. Then we need each other's wisdom and discernment, and we also need each other's prayers.

Several years ago, I felt inspired to write a novel. When publishers rejected it, I lost heart and poured out my feelings to the Lord. I was surprised by what I thought he said. I took it to two praying friends, asking them to sit with me and enquire of the Lord about my writing. It was amazing when they received words and pictures corroborating what I had heard, and I understood that I had, indeed, heard the Lord. But to fully understand the message, I needed believing friends.

Samuel went on to hear God's message, and though it was shocking and harsh, he relayed it all to Eli. He was a faithful witness and messenger of what God entrusted to him. An active, working relationship developed between God and Samuel, and he proved to be a reliable prophet.

Father, thank you that you know my name. Keep me in the spiritual place to hear your voice and, when the message is unclear, give me the humility to seek the prayerful counsel of others mature in the faith.

MICHELE D. MORRISON

Expecting to hear

So [Rebekah] went to ask the Lord about it. 'Why is this happening to me?' she asked. And the Lord told her. (NLT)

I love the simplicity of this reading. Rebekah asked, and the Lord answered. Ask, and it shall be given to you. Rebekah brought an attitude of expectancy to her prayer, trusting that the Lord would answer her. She was worn out. First, she couldn't conceive, and then, in answer to Isaac's fervent pleading, the Lord blessed them with a pregnancy. But even before birth, her twins tussled. I've never carried twins, but I can imagine that the movement as they struggled for space must have been wearing. Rather than complaining to Isaac, Rebekah had the good sense to take the problem straight to the Lord. 'Why is this happening to me?' she asked, expecting an answer.

And the Lord told her. How? Did she hear an audible voice? Sometimes we assume biblical characters heard God clearly in a way that is not so usual today, whereas people in scripture were humans just like you and me. Hearing God involves expectancy and trust. When we think we hear God's voice, we should ensure it conforms to what the God revealed in Jesus would say. Knowing his character and his teaching are key, and God will confirm his word through scripture or praying believers. Then comes the moment when we must trust and move into his words in faith.

Rebekah's relationship with God was so natural: she asked the Lord and expected an answer. The Lord's words to Rebekah must have been both reassuring and unsettling. I wonder what might have happened had Rebekah taken God's revelation and used it faithfully to pray for sibling love rather than to accept sibling rivalry. Respectful dialogue is part of relationship, but we can only dialogue when we recognise his voice.

Lord, give us the confidence to expect answers from you. May we not be content with silence, but press in to hear you.

MICHELE D. MORRISON

Listen

'Indeed, I stand at the door and knock. If anyone hears my voice and opens the door, I will come in and we will have dinner together.' (The Source)

At 18, I found living in a university hall extremely lonely. My room-mate had a boyfriend to eat dinner with each night. Being shy, I was afraid that if I knocked on the door of any of the girls on the corridor, I might be disturbing them. I hoped that, when I plucked up courage and did knock, I would be invited to go down to share dinner with that girl. Usually I was, but what if, instead, I had been greeted with open arms, invited in and then abandoned as the girl went down to dinner without me?

Jesus confirms here that he is near every one of us, waiting to be invited into our hearts. Judging from the number of people who confess faith at mission events and then fall away, it may be easier to open the door to Jesus than to hang out with him, building relationship 'over dinner', so to speak. Yet what more perfect companion could we have? Meals should be characterised by laughter, joy and good discussion. Our interaction with the Lord should be the same: not a duty, but a pleasure.

Christian mindfulness can help us develop a more receptive attitude for hearing God's voice: sitting still, focusing on the breath, breathing in and out his name, until we've quietened our spirits and expect to hear from God. Or we can focus on a verse of scripture and repeat it slowly, without hurry, staying with it until it sinks into our hearts. Try Psalm 91:1 (NLT): 'Those who live in the shelter of the Most High will find rest in the shadow of the Almighty.'

Jesus wants us to invite him into the intimate places of our lives, so that we can share with him and he can share with us.

Lord Jesus, be at home in my heart, in my mind, in my life. May I be eager to share with you, lingering in your presence and recognising your voice in my heart. I love you, Lord.

MICHELE D. MORRISON

The Bible speaks

You have learnt the sacred scriptures from infancy. This has empowered you to be wise and has led to your salvation through faith in Jesus the Anointed One. All Scripture is made alive by God. (The Source)

We hear God through his living word. Jesus, the Word spoken at creation, became flesh, and through the Spirit he inhabits the written word. I remember how in a period of distress God led me in a miraculous way to Deuteronomy 31:8 to comfort me. He has also led me to scripture to correct me. I was going to a weekend conference and was fasting the day it started. Instead of heading to the dining room for dinner, I knelt at my bedside and asked for a word. I had an impulse to look at Matthew 7, where I read with dismay, 'Do not judge, or you too will be judged' (Matthew 7:1, NIV). There ensued a conversation with God which corrected a bad attitude I hadn't even recognised.

In this passage, Paul teaches Timothy that scripture speaks to us in order to equip us to do good works. If we need a rebuke, as I did, we hear it and, as his Spirit changes us, we become a clearer love letter from God to his world. In the beginning, the Word spoke life into being, and he still does. As we let his word nourish and challenge our deepest beings, he highlights a truth we need for that moment, empowering and equipping us to obey. The writer to the Hebrews says that scripture is sharper than a double-edged sword, even dividing soul and spirit.

As products of our culture and our nurture, our souls are often at odds with the Spirit and need to be transformed into the likeness of Jesus. Thinking as God thinks, having the mind of Christ, can only happen as we listen to God's voice and allow him free rein.

God speaks through the Bible, and he works miracles within us.

Am I surrendered to God in my deepest being? Do I believe that the Bible is truly the word of God, or do I pick and choose my way through it?

MICHELE D. MORRISON

What does God's voice sound like?

And after the earthquake there was a fire, but the Lord was not in the fire. And after the fire there was the sound of a gentle whisper. When Elijah heard it, he wrapped his face in his cloak and went out. (NLT)

Elijah knows God's voice: he is a prophet. It's been a dangerous, arduous struggle, and many times he's had to confront powerful people. He's lived risky faith in his struggle with the priests of Baal and by prophesying the end of the drought (1 Kings 18), trusting God for the impossible, and God has honoured him. Now he's exhausted, and Jezebel's threats undermine him and perhaps even shake his faith.

When Elijah pours out his heart, the Lord doesn't remind him of all the miracles, encouraging him to get back into the fray. Instead, he invites Elijah into a closer encounter with him. God understands our human frailty, and 'will not allow you to be tested beyond your power to remain firm' (1 Corinthians 10:13, GNT). I love the way that God honours Elijah, first by blessing him with a closer encounter than he has previously enjoyed, and then by promoting him off the battlefield and into heaven.

Elijah probably expects the all-powerful God to sound like thunder, to burn like fire and to rock his world like an earthquake. Yet he recognises God is not in those, but in a gentle breeze. How like a loving Father, to embrace and not shake a weary child! A comforting appearance as a gentle wind, and release from service.

Few of us hear God's audible voice, but we can hear his intimate voice, that gentle whisper deep within. Elijah heard the whisper because he was where God wanted him to be, waiting expectantly. We are wise to do the same: wait expectantly in the place of prayer. When Elijah heard the whisper, he covered his face and pulled in closer to God. God's whisper should draw us deeper in, where we are blessed as we linger in his presence.

Don't miss deeper revelation because of an impatient impulse to act immediately. Ask God to help you rest in his presence, making you eager to hear and, like Elijah, brave to obey.

MICHELE D. MORRISON

God's voice through drea

But while Joseph was there in the prison, the Lo
showed him kindness and granted him favour in
warder. (NIV)

I don't dream much, but I once dreamt that I was lyi
bed. Beside me, sleeping soundly, was a lion with a ... mane.
I was afraid I would be Aslan's dinner, so I went to t ... ...dge and got
what I thought was a lump of cheese, though it turned out to be butter!
I brought it to the sleeping lion and waited. Then I awoke, and asked God
what he was saying to me in the dream. So far, my understanding is that,
though I trust God to a point, I am still anxious to appease him with my
offerings. Dreams can be parables: God's voice in story-form.

The teenage Joseph was a show-off, sharing his dreams proudly. Did
he recognise God's voice in his dreams? His brothers and dad didn't like
the implications of Joseph's dream, maybe because they believed they
might be true. Whatever Joseph thought, in the pit and in prison he had
time to remember, reflect and pray. His integrity and nobility under the
most testing of conditions reveal that he knew and trusted God, and perhaps the dreams gave him hope to sustain him.

In my dream, I recognised God's voice but had to go to him for understanding. Joseph had time to grow in wisdom and understanding. He
trusted that God's will is never thwarted, and he was strengthened and
encouraged to keep hoping despite circumstances which could have led
to despair. Through all his tribulations, he relied on God and, in his darkest hour, his spirit was sustained by the conviction that eventually God's
will would prevail. God's voice, through the dreams, comforted, guided
and inspired Joseph through the many trials he suffered.

Sometimes our own dreams die, but the ones from God are
always true.

Do you have any God-given dreams on which you've given up? Maybe it's
time to talk to God about them again.

MICHELE D. MORRISON

voice through visions

not be afraid, you who are highly esteemed,' he said. 'Peace!
be strong now; be strong.' (NIV)

Daniel, like Elijah and Joseph, lived on the edge, staying true to his God despite dwelling in a hostile environment. Perhaps hostility sharpens the appetite for relationship with God.

Daniel fasted for three weeks from things which might have anaesthetised his senses and dulled his spiritual ears, and saw a terrifying vision of the future during an encounter with an angel, who gave him an insight into supernatural realities. The vision had a reach far beyond his individual circumstances.

Repressive regimes are alive and well in our time, too. Christian Solidarity Worldwide (CSW) and other organisations advocate for our sisters and brothers across the globe who are called to be Daniels in this generation. While we lobby for them and encourage them through letter-writing, we are also called to pray that they stand firm under pressure. Through the persecuted church, as through Daniel millennia ago, God's voice booms.

Our enemy is a chameleon, morphing as he seeks to undermine our faith. We may not live where the church is openly persecuted, but political correctness, not scripture, sets the curriculum for what our children are taught. Social norms are increasingly unrestricted. Our enemy dulls our spiritual ears through the noise of the world. We must pray like Daniel, steadfastly, sacrificially and patiently, and, as we wait, God will speak to us and through us. May we be eager to hear his voice and be empowered by the Spirit to be brave.

We are not all prophets, but we can all try to hear and pass on encouraging prophetic words when we receive them. God is always speaking encouragement, hope and strength to his people: as you wait on him, he will use you as his mouthpiece.

Father, thank you for Daniel's extraordinary prayer life and for his relationship with you. May I persevere in prayer as I see a world in turmoil and trouble. Help me to hear your voice.

MICHELE D. MORRISON

God's voice through angels

The Messenger answered, 'I am Gabriel, who stands in the presence of God, and who was sent to announce this Good News to you!... Every spoken word from God has power.' (The Source)

Dr Ann Nyland, translator of The Source New Testament, chooses 'messenger' for the word usually translated 'angel'. This passage encompasses two spectacular visits from Gabriel to announce the births of two very special babies. Speaking to a sceptical Zechariah, Gabriel declares, 'I am Gabriel, who stands in the presence of God, and who was sent to announce...' Despite the angel's awesome appearance and credentials, Zechariah doubts his message, and for such hesitation is struck dumb. Mary, however, is willing to accept whatever God gives her, despite the dangers inherent in the message. What inspiring faith! To Mary's confusion over how this promise can be fulfilled, Gabriel says, 'Nothing is impossible for God!' (v. 37, CEV), or 'every spoken word from God has power'. In Genesis 1, every time God speaks, something happens. Nothing is impossible for God. Every spoken word from God has power.

We see angels throughout scripture: warning Abraham, encouraging Elijah, strengthening Daniel, releasing Peter from prison. Magnificence, in terms of size, brightness and ethereal splendour, seems to characterise angelic appearances. Yet the writer to the Hebrews advises his readers not to forget to entertain strangers, 'for by so doing some people have entertained angels without knowing it' (Hebrews 13:2). So not every angelic appearance is supernaturally awesome and extraordinary.

Sometimes, however, it is. I knew a godly woman, Nan, who is now with the Lord. She once experienced what she recognised as a demonic attack in her bedroom and, as she contended, an angel appeared and strengthened her. We have an amazing God, a creative God, a loving God, whose voice speaks in many ways. May we be open to hearing him in ways ordinary and extraordinary.

Father God, may I never close my mind to God-ordained encounters. You are the God of the impossible. Thank you for the ministry of angels.
                                                          MICHELE D. MORRISON

The work of the Holy Spirit

'When the Spirit of truth comes, he will guide you into all truth. He will not speak on his own but will tell you what he has heard… He will bring me glory by telling you whatever he receives from me.' (NLT)

God speaks to his people through the Holy Spirit. It is spiritually presumptuous to claim we hear the voice of God if we are seeking to glorify ourselves or manipulate others. We have a friend who was told by a woman at church that God had told her that he and she would be married. His response was, 'Well, he hasn't told me!'

This passage makes it clear that the Spirit speaks to bring glory to Jesus. He speaks through scripture, through other people, directly into our minds and through events and circumstances.

Hear the love in Jesus' words, 'There is so much more I want to tell you, but you can't bear it now' (v. 12). Through the Spirit, Jesus drip-feeds us. As we mature, our spiritual digestive system matures, enabling us to process increasingly deeper truth. Jesus' statement reveals that some truth is hard for us – we can't bear it. Like a loving parent feeding a toddler, he knows when we are able to feed on the deeper truths.

My daughter does voice-over work from a small studio in her house. Recently, I was visiting while she had a recording session scheduled. Sitting downstairs, I found my ears were sensitive to every car engine, helicopter, street sweeper, even birdsong, and I feared the noise would undermine the quality of her work. Her soundproofed studio muffled the sounds, though, and the session was a success. As I walk through my daily life, I want to become so attentive to God's voice that my faith forms effective soundproofing to the world's interference. As I use social media, I want him to filter out what is fake news and, as I engage with others, I want an inner earpiece tuned to the Father advising me on what to believe.

Lord, forgive me when I choose to ignore the wise guidance you give. Thank you for intervening. Thank you for overruling. Pin my ears back and give me a quiet, loving spirit.

MICHELE D. MORRISON

Jesus builds his church

'In the last days,' God says, 'I will pour out my Spirit upon all people. Your sons and daughters will prophesy. Your young men will see visions, and your old men will dream dreams.' (NLT)

Some commentators identify the period following Jesus' life on earth as 'the last days'. These are our days. Those who love Jesus hear his voice. He speaks truth and life through us into a dark and crazy world.

'Your sons and daughters will prophesy' (v. 17). What does it mean to prophesy? It means to hear what God says, and to speak it out to the audience he indicates. This gift is so important to the church today.

Jesus said he would build his church. The early church was known for its members' love for each other. So should we be known, as we encourage one another. In my Bible study group, we once asked God to give us an encouraging word, individually, for each other. Expectantly, we each listened and we heard from God. The words we shared with one another were amazing. We loved each other more deeply, and we also loved God better. We were encouraged as we practised recognising the voice of God for each other. Sharing God's words builds his church.

Years ago, my prayer partner and I got busy praying for a video shop to go out of business; we didn't like the look of its videos. God laid it on my heart one night, 'Go in and tell him Jesus loves him' – a message of encouragement. I drew back in horror, stricken with a Jonah complex! This wasn't me. I didn't take the nearest ship headed for Spain, but I did delay. After three weeks of disobedience, I finally went in. When Vincent, the owner of the shop, said, 'I'd have understood the message if you'd come in three weeks ago: the anniversary of my wife's death,' I was thoroughly ashamed of myself. Failing to share the word God gives you hurts others and cripples his church.

Lord, forgive me when my own self-image and discomfort give me lockjaw. May I be bold, obedient and full of love. Fill my mouth with your words, in Jesus' name and for his sake.

MICHELE D. MORRISON

Hard hearts are deaf to God's voice

'Today when you hear his voice, don't harden your hearts as Israel did when they rebelled, when they tested me in the wilderness.' (NLT)

Don't harden your heart. The story of my disobedience that I told yesterday offers a picture of what it looks like to harden your heart. I was more aware of my own self-image than I was of God's character. In my self-righteousness, I focused on the video content; God focused on Vincent. To God, he wasn't a faceless shopkeeper; he was Vincent. God knew Vincent's heart was broken, and that he was empty and open and searching for God. As we gathered a small team to share the word with him, I watched, humbled and penitent, as God worked.

Our spiritual ears are in our hearts; hard hearts are deaf to God's voice. They harden as our vision narrows and we make selfish choices. Repentance is the medicine that softens hearts and restores hearing.

Today is when you hear his voice. God's desire is for relationship with us, and communication builds relationship. Sometimes the noise of the world, of daily life, dulls our spiritual hearing. Sometimes we assume false humility and claim that we are not good enough to hear God's voice. Well, of course we're not: none of us is. But God still speaks to us – that's grace. The disciples on the road to Emmaus on Easter night did not recognise Jesus. But later, after they did, they said with great conviction, 'Didn't our hearts burn within us *as he talked with us*?' (Luke 24:32).

For a fortnight, we've been studying some biblical examples and life lessons on hearing the voice of God. Do you recall times in your life when your heart burned within you, and you recognised he was speaking? Don't we long for that to be our daily experience?

Lord Jesus Christ, you who would never break a bruised reed, forgive me when I am so concerned with myself that I ignore your voice within. Help me to love you more every day.

MICHELE D. MORRISON

Just ask

'Keep on asking, and you will receive what you ask for. Keep on seeking, and you will find. Keep on knocking, and the door will be opened to you.' (NLT)

Jesus, the radiance of God's glory and the exact representation of his being, reveals that the almighty God is a good God. Scripture says that 'the letter [of the law] kills, but the Spirit gives life' (2 Corinthians 3:6, NIV). It says, 'Draw near to God, and he will draw near to you' (James 4:8, NRSV). We have so many promises that reveal a God who is passionate about his creation, a God who walked and talked with the first couple in the cool of the evening. He was not a demanding deity; he was a friend sharing some 'down time' after work.

Be intentional as you seek God. Get a journal: ask God what he sees when he looks at you and write down the first thing that comes to mind. If it's negative, I would suggest you've listened to your own voice. God loves you and he whispers to you with loving words. As Kris Vallotton of Bethel Church says, he 'calls out the gold'.

Give God time and ask him what is on his heart. He may give you a picture, which you may not understand. Jesus taught in parables which weren't always understood immediately, but when asked, he explained. During a church prayer time, I had a picture for a lady sitting opposite me. I shared it with her afterwards. We discussed, through email, what certain things might mean, and it became evident that the Lord was not calling her out into a new ministry but was encouraging and blessing her in her existing ministry of hospitality. As we explored the picture together, the message became clear.

In this age of social media, we have added means, when we hear God's voice, of encouraging one another and exploring what he is saying and new opportunities for spreading God's news of rescue and redemption. Hear what the Lord is saying to you and speak it out.

Lord God, be glorified in my actions, in my words and in my mind. Inspire me and draw me closer to you day by day. Give me a love for your world and make me a channel of your peace.

MICHELE D. MORRISON

James: a practical guide

Sara Batts writes:

This week, we will be reading the letter of James. It's short and relatively easy to read, so I encourage you to read all five chapters, not just the extracts we focus on each day.

James is a bit of a Marmite letter – you either love it or hate it. It was famously called an 'epistle of straw' by Martin Luther for its lack of references to the resurrection and its emphasis on justification by works, rather than by faith alone. And indeed, the focus of James isn't what Christ did for us in his death and resurrection, but what we should do in response to this. I think we can learn much from James' reminder of the practical consequences of deciding to follow Jesus. James may not explicitly give a lesson in God's plan of salvation but where he asks us to act in a certain way, it is because that mirrors the character of God. So we do get to understand more about God, alongside an assessment of our own way of life.

Unlike most of Paul's correspondence, James was not written in response to a specific set of circumstances. It's counted as wisdom literature by some – like Proverbs – because it contains collections of pastoral advice. These sayings parallel those in the gospels of Matthew and Luke, which suggests there might be a common source that all three writers used. It was most likely written to be circulated among Christian communities outside Palestine, to be sent to readers familiar with Christian teaching – but who weren't putting their faith into practice. James writes with love and encouragement, not just commands, and uses metaphors to help us understand his point. That makes it a rich but relatively easy read.

Many hold that the letter was written by James, the brother of Jesus. Some think it was written as early as AD45. The evidence isn't conclusive, but whoever the author was, and whenever the epistle was written, what we have is a guide to life that is as relevant today as it was to those first Christians. The first-century believers progressing to a mature faith needed a distinctively Christian way to work out their problems – and so do we.

Working wholeheartedly

But when you ask, you must believe and not doubt, because the one who doubts is like a wave of the sea, blown and tossed by the wind. (NIV)

Let's start this week with one of the verses that has the potential to scupper our whole reading together. I think we need to look carefully at the language here. We're told in verse 5 that God gives to all generously and without finding fault. This is a comforting echo of Jesus' promise that prayer can move mountains (Matthew 21:21). Yet in verse 8, we read that a doubter must not expect to receive anything.

This verse has a huge potential to create hurt and fear. The yawning chasm of an unanswered plea prayed from desperate circumstances can't be bridged with a simplistic answer, that 'you doubted, so it didn't happen'. I know, because I've been on the painful receiving end of that kind of apparent wisdom. It shreds whatever trust in God we were clinging to.

The Greek word for 'doubt' that's used here does *not* imply a lack of faith in Christ. What it does suggest is division within ourselves, a dispute between our loyalties – which is why James' metaphor of wind-driven waves works so well.

Being divided in our soul means we are at the beck and call of the things we put ahead of Christ. We are like the waves tossed from one side to another by the wind. I have the idea now that perhaps the purpose of James is to help us joyously surf in the tide, riding the high waves in the assurance of God's love for us.

If James' epistle is to be read as a guide to living and growing as a Christian, then what he asks us to do is recognise these internal disputes and to understand that our lives will not show fruit unless we are wholehearted in putting our love for God first.

Heavenly Father, help me to understand myself more this week. Help me live, pray and love with my whole heart focused on you.

SARA BATTS

Working in community

Everyone should be quick to listen, slow to speak and slow to become angry. (NIV)

A letter written centuries ago still holds sage advice for us in our fast-paced, connected world. If you've ever sent an angry email in haste, you'll know the effects that James is warning us about. Even if we've never posted social media comments, we're probably seen or heard among friends the fallout from Facebook posts that become angry arguments. What could be a useful exchange of news and ideas, keeping us in contact with friends and relatives, becomes poisoned by conflict.

One theme I want to draw out from James' letter is how Christian living places us into a community – not just of believers, but also the community beyond our church walls. The idea of being part of a community can be difficult when we are so used to society being oriented around individuals' needs and wants. James understood this. Note that he addresses 'everyone' – we are all exhorted to be slow to anger, slow to speak and quick to listen.

Good listening relies on us being focused on what the other is saying, not jumping to get in with our response. Understanding other people only happens through really hearing their point of view. The feeling of being listened to is the start of reconciliation. Yet anger stops us listening completely – to others, to ourselves, to God.

As a result of life lived with a sense of community, we notice the needs of those around us. While we may not expressly see widows and orphans, caring for those in distress is very much still part of our participation in community. We have a collective responsibility. Listening with understanding to those who struggle with low incomes, disability or other things that lead to marginalisation helps us to know how to relieve the distress of isolation and bring everyone into fullness of life.

Loving God, you hear me when I pray. I pray that I might give others the same attention that you give me, and that when I speak today my words will be words of peace and love.

SARA BATTS

Working for our neighbour

You do well when you complete the Royal Rule of the Scriptures: 'Love others as you love yourself.' (MSG)

Today, we look at another example that is still relevant in the world today. To whom do we give precedence and respect? I think we are likely to welcome the person in fine clothes, and to quietly ignore the other. I think newspaper headlines encourage us to assume that wealth is a mark of good character, and those who are poor deserve their fate.

I think that distinctions created between different groups of people make it hard for us to appreciate who our neighbour really is. Perhaps your church is proud of its children's work and has a thriving family culture. How does it welcome the single elderly person? Or perhaps you're in a church where a child worshipping God would be expected to sit quietly? Maybe you enthusiastically support the food bank, but shy away from drug rehabilitation. Every time we put someone in the category of 'other', we show the kind of partiality that James warns against. Every time we pay attention to those with wealth at the expense of those in poverty, we create a distinction. And what's more – we probably miss out on friendship and wisdom. After all, God has chosen the poor to be rich in faith, says James.

Scripture commands us to love our neighbour as we love ourselves. Who is our neighbour? The simple answer is 'everyone' – and we are back at the idea that our life as a Christian makes us part of a connected whole. The decisions I make with my money and my choice of housing, school or transport have implications for other people. And scripture also wants us to love and accept ourselves. If I do not truly believe I am worthy of love, how can I love others?

Where do you spend your money? Do the businesses you support pay the workers a fair wage, for example? How might the financial decisions you make have an impact on your global neighbours?

SARA BATTS

...ut our faith

...hat God-talk without God-acts is outrageous
(...5)

We saw ...onday how living as a Christian gives us a place in a community, and how that comes with collective responsibilities. In today's passage, James spells this out loud and clear. In his desire to see new Christians mature, he repeats the fundamental idea that faith that is not lived out in our actions is dead.

It reminds me of a conversation I once had about the Lord's Prayer. We pray, 'Your will be done.' I asked, 'Who is it that God uses to shape his will on earth, if not us?' The answer I got implied that people believed there's some miraculous way that God's will is carried out and we're not part of it. I think James here is correcting that view. It is pious but unhelpful to tell someone in need of warmth and food to 'go in peace' if it leaves them cold and hungry. Prayer is important – we should regularly hold the needs of the world before God. But praying isn't the whole story; believing in God isn't the whole story – as James says, even the demons believe in God!

The story of Rahab can be found in Joshua 2. She hid spies sent to scope out Jericho before the Israelites took possession of the land God had promised. James counts her as righteous for this deed, done in the fear of the Lord. It might seem odd that a prostitute's actions – betraying her city – are seen as an example of works that bring faith to life. I think James wants us to see how her motivation is important. Rahab took a risk, because she put God's will first; and she is recognised as having a significant part in Israel's history. We too should take a risk, finding out God's will and joining in with his work.

Loving God, as I pray today, 'Your will be done,' I pray that I will find my way to do your will on earth. Show me, Lord, where my talents and time can be put to your use, and help me live out my faith today.

SARA BATTS

Working with our words

Likewise, the tongue is a small part of the body, but it makes great boasts. Consider what a great forest is set on fire by a small spark. (NIV)

Sometimes, when I am in a stressful situation and I begin to speak, I know the sentence won't end well. Part of my brain is screaming at me to stop, but the speaking part just carries on regardless. Oh, for control over my tongue! Usually it's just a joke that I know is about to fall flat, but it has happened that I've said things that were hurtful, sarcastic or just mean. No amount of apology can fix the hurt caused by a tongue running away with itself.

At least we know it's not just us. James is pretty clear that we all mess up sometimes. Our unbridled tongue gets us into all sorts of trouble. His comparison with a small rudder on a large ship is instructive – showing us just what control over our words can do. Today's passage enlarges on the ideas we met on Monday that if we don't think before we speak, we can do untold damage.

If you've ever been the victim of rumours or gossip, you will well know the hurt they cause; a story misremembered and retold can spread out of all proportion, just like a forest fire. Have you ever shared news under the guise of sharing it 'for prayer', when in any other circumstances it would just be gossip? These things are tempting, but they damage our communities. Conversely, not speaking out in the face of injustice is damaging. We should watch our words out of love, not out of fear of speaking up.

What is the solution? The wisdom from above – the wisdom from God – that has no partiality or hypocrisy is the foundation on which we should build our lives. Then we may find ways to use our words for good.

Let's use our words well today. Find ways to compliment or encourage others you meet. Speak to a stranger; share a joke with a child; call a friend.

SARA BATTS

Working in the world

Draw near to God, and he will draw near to you. (NRSV)

One of the unavoidable things about living as a Christian is that it will sometimes put us at odds with the rest of society. The classic film *Chariots of Fire* tells the story of Eric Liddell, who refused to run qualifying races on a Sunday at the 1924 Olympics. Our conflicts might not be as dramatic as that – and we almost certainly haven't committed murder to get something we want (v. 2)! But James tells us that we cannot be friends with the world and friends with God.

We looked on Sunday at the idea of divided loyalties within ourselves, and here James returns to that idea.

I wonder what we might have *metaphorically* killed to get what we want. Have we put material gain ahead of our family and friendships? Has our desire to earn a higher salary taken priority over our time for God and for the things that root us in community? Or perhaps you're living with a low income, and the stress that entails kills the space for prayer and peacefulness.

James wanted his readers to live a distinctively Christian life. That isn't easy – it wasn't for those first Christians, and it isn't for us in today's climate, immersed in a world that demands friendship on its terms, measuring our worth by our income or our school grades or the size of our house.

Longing for the material goods, the things that the world values, divides our loyalty and takes our focus from our faith. We're back to being tossed about on the stormy seas. Our identity lies in our relationship with Jesus, not the approval of our neighbours. 'Draw near to God,' says James, 'and he will draw near to you' (v. 8). Our way of living, if rooted in our faith, gives us an anchor.

Heavenly Father, I thank you that I am valued by you for who I am, not what I own. I thank you for your assurance that when I seek you, you will draw close to me and help anchor me in my life of faith.

SARA BATTS

Working in prayer

Therefore confess your sins to one another, and pray for one another, so that you may be healed. (NRSV)

James reminds us today of what it means to be accountable, and to live and work alongside others. I don't think he's just referring to Sundays when he envisages a space where the cheerful sing and the suffering pray, where the sick are anointed and sins are forgiven. We should, he says, confess our sins to one another and pray for each other. This is a way for communities to grow to maturity in faith.

The practice of confession may not be part of your tradition but, even if you've ever just had to own up to a mistake at work or home, you will have some sense of how deeply discomforting this can be.

Making a confession means we have to examine ourselves honestly and articulate to someone else the things of which we're most ashamed. We find our gloss and excuses fall away in the light of truthful assessment of our conduct. We note too that if we have this as a regular practice, we return to confess the mundane more often than the sensational. The Anglican Church says of confession: 'all may, some should, none must'. Having a confidential space in which to express our failings, be prayed for and receive assurance of God's forgiveness can be a deeply healing thing. James knew this; he expected his communities of Christians to confess their sins and hear others' admission of faults, and to pray for each other so that they may be healed. We long to see lives healed as the burden of sin and failing is removed; communities healed as trust is earned between people; egos healed as the vulnerable are held gently in prayer; lives and souls healed. In a true community, those who wander are reconciled to the truth.

Heavenly Father, I have sinned and fallen short of your glory. Give me the strength I need to acknowledge my faults. Give me the courage to sing your joyful praise in the knowledge of your forgiveness as I live out my faith.

SARA BATTS

oy of spiritual
iplines

Fiona Barnard writes:

You have fallen for an Italian; he is wonderful. You walk on air and feel giddy. As the relationship deepens, you realise that what is brilliant might be even better if you could speak Italian, the language of love, the dialect of his heart. You pay for a night class. You buy a textbook. You practise over months and years. You commit for the long haul. And, although you never enjoyed grammar and vocabulary at school, now you want to learn exactly that. Love is the key. It is worth all the pain, because it helps you understand your beloved and bask in his affection. It enables you to belong to the new family.

How do we learn the love language of God? Spiritual disciplines are the way God enables us to hear him and speak his language. Through them, he whispers his heart's desires and shapes us. We learn how to belong to his family.

Before he died, Jesus' plea and encouragement to his disciples was urgent: 'I am the vine; you are the branches. If you remain in me and I in you, you will bear much fruit… Now remain in my love' (John 15:5, 9, NIV). They would have wondered 'How?', especially as he was leaving them. We may think, 'In my head I understand I belong to God. But in my everyday life, how do I know the Father, honour the Son and walk in the Spirit?'

Spiritual disciplines are nutrients in the soil of faith. They enable the seed of love to grow. They feed our branches, transforming us so that we can be fruitful. They keep us close to the master gardener and a part of a vineyard extending across the world.

'Keep on working with fear and trembling to complete your salvation, because God is always at work in you to make you willing and able to obey his own purpose' (Philippians 2:12–13, GNT).

Spiritual disciplines give us the food, the language for relationship with our lovely Lord. They develop in us the muscle to work with him in his vineyard.

Prayer

One thing I asked of the Lord, that I will seek after: to live in the house of the Lord all the days of my life, to behold the beauty of the Lord... 'Come,' my heart says, 'seek his face!' Your face, Lord, do I seek. (NRSV)

Recently, our church leaders called us to 40 days of prayer. Initially, the intention was to draw us together to seek God's guidance as we faced a time of transition. However, what has developed is a call to something deeper: to come first to our Father in humility, repentance and dependence. We sense this will prepare us to consider our relationships and church vision. As I write, there are only 20 days to go; we have no idea yet where God will take us on this journey.

Millions of words have been written and spoken on prayer but, at its heart, prayer is very simple. It is seeking God's face. It is beholding his beauty. We are invited into the presence of a Father who longs to spend time with us. We are granted access to his heart through the Lord Jesus. We are given words by the Holy Spirit within us. Responding to God is the most natural thing in the world. So often, we fall effortlessly into prayer when we call out for ourselves or others. We watch the news and cry, 'How long, Lord?' We lose our temper and plead, 'Have mercy, Lord!' We bite into a succulent strawberry and whisper, 'Thank you, Lord!' Yet prayer is also costly. It demands everything in us: discipline, persistence, time, focus, faith.

I am delighted that my church recognises that we have different personalities. So, although the challenge is to everyone, there are various ways to engage in prayer: meditating on a short verse, colouring a sketch, studying longer biblical texts, using visual and tactile prayer stations, creating crafts, walking, sharing in groups, fasting and journalling. Alone and together. Speaking. Listening. Loving. Waiting. But it is all about one thing: seeking God's beautiful face.

I read about an Iraqi Christian who had lost everything because of her faith in Christ. Psalm 27 was her favourite psalm. Pray it with her and for her and others who suffer persecution.

FIONA BARNARD

Worship

Praise the Lord, my soul; all my inmost being, praise his holy name… who forgives… and heals… and crowns you with love and compassion… The Lord works righteousness and justice for all the oppressed… he does not treat us as our sins deserve… He remembers that we are dust. (NIV)

It was as though God had collected all the reds and oranges and yellows in his celestial paint pot and poured them into the heavens. He'd rubbed his finger in great swirls around the clouds and just kept touching up the shifting display of exquisite glory. I'd just turned a corner and stopped, stunned in awe. On an evening like that, worship was a spontaneous response to an extravagant creator. For those with eyes to see, beauty which points to our God is everywhere and gives fuel to our praise.

At other times, in the absence of splendour, worship is adjusting the magnet of our life's compass so that it points us to the Lord. In adoration, we express truths we may not feel at the time, but upon which we stake our lives. It is good to make gratitude a habit, as we encounter his hand in the ordinary.

We also need the encouragement of gathering with God's people to celebrate who he is and what he has done for us. For me, helpful congregational worship will take me on a journey from distraction and fretting to focus and encounter: 'The Lord is compassionate and gracious, slow to anger, abounding in love' (v. 8). These words have served as life-giving liturgy through millennia of faith and worship.

Last weekend, I was at a seminar on the use of Godly Play with preschoolers. Most moving were the children's responses as they not only heard a Bible story, but entered into a sense of holy awe, touching and smelling and feeling what was happening before them. As the teller asked 'I wonder' questions which have no prescribed answer, faith and love and 'wow' stirrings were given space to grow.

Why, oh why, do adults so easily leave wonder behind?

Worshipping God for his character and praising him for what he has done go together. Why not spend a few minutes pondering reasons to give him thanks today? Let Psalm 103 inspire you.

FIONA BARNARD

Journalling

I said, 'God, God-of-Heaven, the great and awesome God, loyal to his covenant and faithful to those who love him and obey his commands: Look at me, listen to me. Pay attention to this prayer of your servant that I'm praying day and night in intercession for your servants.' (MSG)

The compulsive need to capture my life in words started in my teenage years. Writing itself became therapy, my tears and tales washing up on the page. Daily diaries and journals developed into ways of noting God's dealings with me as he spoke and guided. In the struggle to understand what I think and how to pray, I have discovered my heart's desire in the forming of sentences and ideas.

I often think of the book of Nehemiah as a journal. In the busyness of managing the rebuilding of Jerusalem's walls, Nehemiah needed time to reflect on what was happening. In the face of opposition from Israel's enemies and complaints within God's people, he laid his motives and actions before the Lord: 'Remember me with favour, my God, for all I have done for these people' (5:19, NIV). Looking back, he brought moments of fury to God: 'Remember them, my God, because they defiled the priestly office and the covenant of the priesthood and of the Levites' (13:29, NIV). He recalled God's faithfulness in a community prayer: 'You are a forgiving God, gracious and compassionate, slow to anger and abounding in love' (9:17, NIV). He relived days of celebration when he told the people, 'The joy of the Lord is your strength' (8:10, NIV). Writing helped him process experiences, clarify decisions and discern God's call and direction.

Nehemiah's journal was a personal way of praying, capturing an event, releasing an emotion. It also became a memoir for his grandchildren to enjoy. On a scale he could never have imagined, it resulted in a record of faithful dependence on God, wise leadership and commitment to teamwork which has inspired and instructed God's people through the centuries.

If you don't journal already, how about starting?

FIONA BARNARD

Confession

If we walk in the light, as he is in the light, we have fellowship with one another, and the blood of Jesus, his Son, purifies us from all sin... If we confess our sins, he is faithful and just and will forgive us our sins and purify us from all unrighteousness. (NIV)

'Another pencil case has disappeared from the classroom corridor.' I still feel my insides somersault as I recall the stern head teacher's announcements at repeated school assemblies. It was quite ludicrous: first, that so many were vanishing, but second, the gut sense that I must be the culprit. Through the years, I have come to realise that my conscience plays tricks on me: it can be both falsely guilty and stubbornly deaf.

It is for this very reason that confession is such a necessary discipline. Along with fellow sinners, we need the regular public admission of our evil thoughts, words and deeds. When we come to the Lord's supper, we visualise the sin that nailed Jesus to the cross. We must acknowledge our selfishness and greed if we are to keep close to Christ. In a place where grace is poured out, we name not only vague misdemeanours, but the specific wrongs that shame us and wound the heart of God. And we leave them there in sorrow and resolve to change. We discover afresh that only in true confession can we know the depth of Jesus' salvation.

Sometimes, when a general guilty feeling swirls round me like a fog without settling on anything specific, although I recognise the hand of the accuser, I am left defeated and hopeless, far from the Father's forgiving embrace. Then the compassionate listening of a fellow Christian helps me discern false allegations. At other times, when I imagine that the heinousness of my offence can never be pardoned, the careful acceptance of a trusted fellow believer brings Jesus' healing. Then, when self-reproach terrorises me, I can say, 'I confessed all the mess and muck to Jesus and to her. I heard words of absolution: I am forgiven because of Jesus' death for me. Hallelujah!'

'This is how we know that we belong to the truth and how we set our hearts at rest in his presence: if our hearts condemn us, we know that God is greater than our hearts, and he knows everything' (1 John 3:19–20, NIV).

FIONA BARNARD

Communion

Jesus, on the night of his betrayal, took bread. Having given thanks, he broke it and said, 'This is my body, broken for you. Do this to remember me.' After supper, he did the same thing with the cup: 'This cup is my blood, my new covenant with you. Each time you drink this cup, remember me.' (MSG)

There have been many times in my life when I have felt so unworthy that I have not taken part in Communion. These days, I usually do. Not because I have become more holy, but because my focus has changed: the Lord's supper is not primarily about me and my relationship with God. It is about what Jesus has done. It is about being part of his body.

So now, I savour the taste of mystery as I join people going forward to take bread and wine: the stroppy teenager, the stooping granny, the reserved head teacher and the 'only just together' first-time parent. I stand with them at the cross which towers across time. I pause to gaze afresh at the depths of agony Jesus endured instead of us. I become acutely aware of physicality: the bread and wine I am swallowing, the body and blood of Jesus, his life and death which I am taking into my very muscles and bones. I sense the body of Christ around me and the body of Christ throughout the world in huts, cathedrals, catacombs and house churches. I glimpse the breadth of Christ's arms of mercy thrown open to us across seas and through centuries. I am awed by the new life we share through his Spirit. I am part of something much bigger: a family, a community. And despite our failures, which bring us back repeatedly to this cross and this meal, we are his powerful advertisement of hope and reconciliation.

Communion is a communal reminder of what is central to our faith: love, sacrifice, invitation, worship, repentance, gratitude, body. Our sins make us eligible. Our swallowing makes us humble. Our partaking makes us one in Christ. Hallelujah!

Next time you are at a Communion service, look at your brothers and sisters, including the ones you don't like, and praise God for the miracle of this new community. Thank him for what he did to make it possible.

FIONA BARNARD

Hospitality

'When you give a dinner or a banquet, don't invite your friends and family and relatives and rich neighbours. If you do, they will invite you in return, and you will be paid back. When you give a feast, invite the poor, the crippled, the lame, and the blind… God will bless you.' (CEV)

'Can you tell us about the time you went to your friend's house for a meal and she gave you three tomatoes?' My nieces love hearing about one of my stranger hospitality experiences. They are so used to lasagne and meatballs, pavlovas and Victoria sponges that the vision of disappointed hope tickles them greatly.

What is significant for me in this story is not the menu (just as well!), but the invitation. Sara had a mental illness which often made her hide away. She was painfully thin, many times forgetting to eat. Yet on this occasion, she wanted to open her home and offer what she had to us. It involved huge effort on her part and demonstrated a generosity of spirit. That touched us. (The feast was later supplemented by one cup-a-soup and, thankfully, a resourceful neighbour rescued the day with an omelette.) We also had a great time together, chatting on a level not always possible during after-church fellowship.

It's appealing that when God lived on earth in Christ, he came 'eating and drinking'. That was where friendships were made, stories were told and barriers broken down. In God's creative design, when we share food, we share our lives. As we munch our carrots, we chew ideas and dreams. When we taste bread and wine, we savour the Lord's kindness to us.

To sharpen our appetites for the great celestial banquet, the wedding feast of Christ and his bride, the church, we are encouraged to practise hospitality. It may come more naturally to some than to others, so 'practise' is a heartening word. When we focus on welcoming others, whether with gourmet delights or a disaster surprise, a bag of chips or three tomatoes, we mirror Jesus. We give more than food; we celebrate God's bounteous nourishment.

Is there someone this week with whom you could share a coffee or a simple meal?

FIONA BARNARD

Simplicity

'Steep your life in God-reality, God-initiative, God-provisions. Don't worry about missing out. You'll find all your everyday human concerns will be met.' (MSG)

Visiting the poor in Brazilian slums was a regular feature of my childhood weekend. I recall the misery and despair, the stench of open sewers and the sense that life was not fair. My parents' engagement in the physical and spiritual health of many was a drop in the ocean of need. Returning to the comparatively affluent UK was a massive shock. My response was to be mean with my money and critical about the spending of others. To my thinking, the Bible was quite unambiguous about greed and selfishness, and I thought I could see through all the excuses the wealthy liked to make.

Years later, a friend decided to celebrate her 40th birthday at an expensive restaurant. Unable to bear the outrageous cost of the meal, I did not respond to the invitation. And then the Lord began to probe: 'Has your thrift become an idol? Is money now more important to you than relationships?' There was more: 'Has your hoarding because you cannot throw anything out actually complicated your life? Has your clutter and judgemental attitude distracted you from what is most important?'

Simplicity is about being free of acquisitiveness, asceticism and addiction, so that we can concentrate wholly on one thing: God's kingdom. Jesus shows us the way. He points to the beauty of wildflowers and bounty of bird lunch! Revelling in God's gifts in creation, he then urges his disciples to 'give him first place in your life and live as he wants you to' (v. 33, TLB). It is a challenge to live responsibly without holding too tightly to possessions. Only a single-minded and continuous focus on Jesus' kingdom priorities will guide us. Simple living is a response of gratitude and trust. It frees our heart, our time and our interactions with others to be like Christ.

Lord, my life is so full of stuff, I am often worried and distracted. Please show me your way!

FIONA BARNARD

Generosity

I am completely satisfied with the gifts that you had Epaphroditus bring me. They are like a sweet-smelling offering or like the right kind of sacrifice that pleases God. I pray that God will take care of all your needs with the wonderful blessings that come from Christ Jesus! (CEV)

It was one of the highlights of my trip to Ghana. 'Now we are going to dance the offering,' announced a usually staid minister. 'And as our Ghanaian friends are visiting, they can show us how.' I clenched my limbs determinedly to the pew as 20 beaming Africans leapt up and began to jive their way to the front. Swaying to the drum beat, they deposited their gifts with a flourish in two big baskets and circled the congregation. To my astonishment, led by their pastor, the elderly Presbyterians grabbed their Zimmer frames and handbags and skipped up the aisle. Even after returning to their seats, they continued hopping, as though the freedom to celebrate God's goodness had got the better of their respectability. 'Come on,' my friend urged me. 'Let's do it.'

Our God is so extravagant in his kindness. Life and breath, beauty and colour, family and friendship, food and fun all come from his brimming generosity. When we experience his care, his salvation, his encouragement, how else can we respond but in the sort of gratitude that gets us off our seats in glad (and pulsing and self-forgetful) surrender?

Stewardship is where we demonstrate our long-term resolve to respond with all that we are to all we have received from our loving Father. It is easy to sing 'Take my life', because that can be woolly and general. We really mean it when we put those notes in the offering; when we devote a morning to weeding our neighbour's garden; when we turn off the TV in order to tune in to someone's story we've heard a hundred times. That is when we show Jesus we mean it: in open-handedness with our money, time and skills. That is how we share his generous and infectious joy.

The Philippians' gift to Paul touched him greatly as he sat in prison. The care of Epaphroditus added to his sense of being blessed. Thoughtfulness matters.

FIONA BARNARD

Partnership

For Christ's love compels us, because we are convinced that one died for all, and therefore all died. And he died for all, that those who live should no longer live for themselves but for him who died for them and was raised again… We are therefore Christ's ambassadors. (NIV)

Our team had just finished a hearty breakfast of pizza and doughnuts. The Romanian church members, who had hosted us with such generosity and kindness, arrived to send us on our way home. Not many were confident English speakers, and our Romanian amounted to about three sentences. How could we convey what we felt? 'Let's sing,' someone said. 'Let's sing, "Bind Us Together, Lord".' Haltingly, we began, and suddenly, like a great wave of energy, our friends grabbed our hands, hauled us to our feet and joined in. The language barrier dissolved. Looking round at the faces of those I had only known a few days, I felt a deep bond. We had been partners in mission, sharing in outreach to kids and adults. Here, together, brothers and sisters in Christ, we were praising the one who had gathered us into his family. It was a foretaste of heaven.

If we want to enter into the fullness of who God is and what he has done, we need to expand our horizons. The Lord is king over the whole earth and he longs to kiss the nations. The beauty of a diamond in sunlight is that it reflects a rainbow of colours. The splendour of the Son's salvation is most brilliant in local multicultural churches which care passionately for those from every tribe, tongue and people.

The nations come to us for work and study, and as visitors and refugees. Let us be the first to welcome them. And the call still rings out for those who will cross the seas to be part of God's mission worldwide. Whether going, giving or praying, being in a team is God's way. In participating, our faith is strengthened and God's kingdom is built. And you might even get pizza and doughnuts for breakfast!

What is your part in touching the nations with the love and truth of Jesus?
                                                                    FIONA BARNARD

Sabbath rest

[Jesus] said, 'The Son of Man is no slave to the Sabbath; he's in charge... Let me ask you something: What kind of action suits the Sabbath best? Doing good or doing evil? Helping people or leaving them helpless?' (MSG)

When I was a child, I had a Sunday box. In it were my elite toys and most recently acquired books and games. While I enjoyed other dolls and knick-knacks the rest of the week, these had special charm on Sundays. Play felt fresher somehow, and my novel amusements gave the day an exciting feel. Time spent in these activities brought something different out in me and my companions. I am grateful to my parents for showing me the delightful uniqueness of the first day of the week.

We live in a mad world of timetables and tiredness, busyness and burnout, addiction and anxiety. Our bodies and minds cry out in protest, 'We are not machines. Give us a break!' So often, we ignore them amid the screaming demands around us. Yet God has gifted us with this day to pause and rest, to cease from doing stuff and just be ourselves. We are human *be*-ings (not *do*-ings); worshippers; members of families and communities. Contrary to popular opinion, if I stop for a day the world will not shudder to a halt, the shops will not run out of stock and the email inbox will not explode with overload.

Once a week, we are given the opportunity to step back and focus afresh on our loving Father; to share with others the gifts of food and laughter; to tell the stories of Jesus; to reorient our priorities; to breathe in the air of God's Spirit; to revel in his creation brimming over with colour and texture and shapes. This is his Sunday box, given to thrill and renew, to bring joy and to strengthen relationships. But we need to open it. We must set the other gadgets aside. As we make it a non-negotiable rhythm of our week, we discover God's goodness overflowing to the other six days.

Use Psalm 92, 'A Sabbath Song', to proclaim the Lord's love and faithfulness.

FIONA BARNARD

Evangelism

Through us, he brings knowledge of Christ. Everywhere we go, people breathe in the exquisite fragrance. Because of Christ, we give off a sweet scent rising to God, which is recognised by those on the way of salvation – an aroma redolent with life. (MSG)

'Saving the world from mediocre coffee': I love the way this well-known coffee chain's mission statement partners the vast panoramic claim with the humble intoxicating coffee! Who can resist the smell of it? My heart does a twirl every time I see those words on the back of a lorry, not only because my Brazilian upbringing taught me that when it comes to coffee, there can be no compromise, but also because the whole notion of 'saving the world' is so expansive, so wonderful, so Christlike. It is what Jesus does, by his life and death, through his church, in the power of the Holy Spirit. Who wants to paddle in mediocrity when you can dive into salvation?

When it comes to evangelism, this is the astounding partnership: Father, Son and Holy Spirit offer salvation to your colleague, your granny, your friend, the family across your street, the refugees and tyrants and farmers across the world. You and I join forces to tell them about it, to show them what it means to live life in all its fullness. We share our lives as we chat in the tea break. We offer lifts, casseroles and time. We support with money and prayer those who travel to spread the message that Jesus is the Saviour of the whole world. We give our lives for Christ's salvation because 'mediocre' has no place in the heartbeat of God's magnificent design.

For many of us, 'evangelism' is a scary word that makes us feel guilty. That is why we are so dependent on the Spirit to give us the heart for those leading 'mediocre' lives (and worse) and the wisdom and opportunities to point them to Christ. And when we take the plunge, we discover that Jesus becomes more precious, his message rings increasingly true and his salvation is exquisitely fragrant and compelling.

Pray for people you know who are good at chatting about Jesus, that they may be encouraged today. Pray that you may have opportunities to spread Christ's sweet-smelling scent wherever he takes you.

FIONA BARNARD

Service

'Whoever wants to be great must become a servant. Whoever wants to be first among you must be your slave. That is what the Son of Man has done: He came to serve, not be served – and then to give away his life in exchange for the many who are held hostage.' (MSG)

The visits my father's carers make four times a day are a sanity-saver for me. I am grateful beyond words. He is so dependent on them, though not really aware of what is happening – but I am. I notice the little things. I see those carers more intent on following social media than the care plan. I detect the ones who do the bare minimum (sloppily). I note those who respond to my father's needs with imagination and willingness. I can tell the ones who are happy to care. Attitude makes all the difference when it seems as though no one sees.

Service is in the Christian's job description, because we follow Jesus, who washed his friends' smelly feet and reached out to the unlovely in compassion. We know it is a response of gratitude and obedience even when we are tired or busy. It is a tricky one, though, because if we show off our good turns or resent those we serve, it sullies our contribution. We may be pulling up weeds for an arthritic pensioner or babysitting an autistic child and, yes, the world will be a better place for our efforts. Yet having a martyr spirit or smug self-righteousness will spoil our volunteering in a charity shop or on the after-church coffee rota.

So when you are up to your elbows in soap suds yet again or that pesky caller rings back with more demands, ask the Lord to work on your heart. Let him shape in you a Christlike humility which can only be expressed and exercised in service. But focus on him, not on your need for affirmation or usefulness. The day will offer many opportunities for little acts of kindness and courtesy if you notice and care, even when no one is looking.

Lord, I love you! Give me someone I can serve today in your name.

FIONA BARNARD

Bible engagement

If you point these things out to the brothers and sisters, you will be a good minister of Christ Jesus, nourished on the truths of the faith and of the good teaching that you have followed… Devote yourself to the public reading of Scripture, to preaching and to teaching. (NIV)

In an age of multiple Bible translations and a plethora of personalised smartphone apps, it is easy to forget that throughout most of Christian history, God's word has been heard in community. The 'you' in the Bible is generally plural rather than singular. Written in a collective culture for a nation or a group, my hunch is that God wants us to hear history, story, poetry, philosophy, wisdom, biography and letter along with our brothers and sisters in Christ. Together we can muse prayerfully, 'What do you make of that? How do you see that working in our community life?'

The Bible comes alive for me when I read it in an international group. I come away more excited about scripture and about a God who speaks to all cultures. 'I'd love to read Ecclesiastes,' whispers a Japanese philosopher, 'if you say it is about the meaning of life. That's what I am looking for.' As we talk about the story of Ruth, an Angolan member chips in, 'That's what happens in some parts of my country. The widow marries her brother-in-law, but often the men are more interested in the sex than having another child for their dead brother. This Boaz seems different. I like him.' Often, I am shaken out of complacency, such as when someone said, 'I don't think Mary and Joseph liked their baby. I mean, why did they put him in a cold hut with the animals?'

In a group, you can take different character parts as you read a story. You can sing a psalm and sit in silence with Job and his friends. You can paint Revelation images, explore the geography of Israel and pray with Paul. Amid disappointment and pain, questioning and joy, you see, touch, taste and feel God's revelation through the Spirit, by his word with each other.

Paul urges a young, timid Timothy to share God's truth in the face of deceit and godless myths. Pray for those tasked with preaching and teaching, for children's church leaders and for Bible study groups in your area.

FIONA BARNARD

Meditation

> They delight in doing everything God wants them to, and day and night are always meditating on his laws and thinking about ways to follow him more closely. They are like trees along a riverbank bearing luscious fruit each season without fail. Their leaves shall never wither. (TLB)

'Lord, make me like a tree!' That is my life's prayer. I love the image of strength and stability, roots going deep. But this is no stuck-in-the-mud, going-nowhere type of living. Swaying branches respond to the wind of the Spirit. There is always something different going on as the season's changing colours tint spectacular leaves. There is lush fruitfulness. There is shelter for weary wanderers escaping the rain. There is an invitation of fun for young adventurers scaling the heights.

A 'tree life' is nurtured by meditating on God's word – letting its goodness sink to the very depths of your being: repeating a verse that has spoken to you, discussing the meaning of a passage with friends, writing notes during a sermon, savouring implications and possibilities, returning to them as you wash the dishes or have a shower. Each person finds their own way when hunger and delight are there. Commentaries and other books are a wonderful resource for more serious study. There are also many outstanding devotional materials that merit time and effort for the sake of our spiritual maturity. Faithful Christians I have never met have shaped my life in numerous significant ways through the printed page.

And in the winter days of struggle, when desire feels dormant, we are fed by other disciplines which point to God's truths: congregational worship, confession, the Lord's supper and sabbath rest. We are encouraged to persevere through prayer and journalling, fellowship and service, mission and hospitality. Trees don't grow in a day. The wonder and relief of being a tree is that our loving Father is the gardener. He is the one who cultivates the life of Jesus in us. The Holy Spirit gathers up our feeble but heartfelt efforts in armfuls. It is a team effort. It is his orchard.

Looking back over the last two weeks, how has God spoken to you?

FIONA BARNARD

The apostle Paul:
Acts 13—28

Lyndall Bywater writes:

I've just learnt a new word. Apparently, 'ballistichory' is the process by which the seed pods on certain plants explode, shooting their seeds far and wide, to ensure the survival of the species. The process occurs because fibres in the casing of the seed pod pull against each other, creating a tension which eventually results in the shell bursting open under force, and its contents being propelled out into the world, sometimes as far as 200 metres away.

Why, you may wonder, have I been researching bursting seed pods? The answer is this: the apostle Paul. We are going to spend the next two weeks in the company of a man who was something of a seed pod for the gospel.

Paul was a man who knew about tension. His first appearance in the book of Acts describes him persecuting Christians – hunting them down to imprison and murder them. His conversion on the Damascus Road wasn't exactly a gentle slide from darkness into light either; quite the opposite, in fact! Jesus seems to have wrestled Paul into the kingdom, arresting him with a ferociously bright light, challenging him on his rebellious ways and then leaving him blind for several days, just in case he thought he might have imagined it all. Then, no sooner was Paul underway with his missionary journeys than he found himself persecuted, tortured, opposed and imprisoned. Trouble often found Paul and, even when it didn't, he frequently went looking for it.

Like those remarkable seed pods, Paul's life was a story of faith under pressure, and that tension created an explosive force which sent seeds far and wide. He saw many churches planted and mentored their leaders. He helped shape the early church's understanding of what the Christian faith was and how it should be lived – and, largely thanks to him, it became a faith in its own right, rather than a sect of Judaism. He brought the good news to the Gentiles; he preached Jesus in the very heart of the Roman empire; and he wrote a bunch of letters which still teach, encourage and inspire believers almost 2,000 years later.

By any estimation, this is a man worth getting to know, and I hope you will enjoy discovering more about him over the coming days.

Self-demotion

While they were worshipping the Lord and fasting, the Holy Spirit said, 'Set apart for me Barnabas and Saul for the work to which I have called them.' (NIV)

George Washington was once riding through the countryside with some friends. As they jumped a wall, one of the horses knocked a few stones off the top. The other riders would have carried on, but George insisted on stopping to repair the damage.

'What are you doing?' asked one of his friends. 'You're too big to be doing that sort of work.'

'On the contrary,' said George, 'I'm just the right size.'

Saul has been in training for ministry, and now he and his friend Barnabas are ready to go. It's perhaps a measure of their first-timer nerves that they head for Paphos, Barnabas' hometown, but if they're hoping for a gentle start, then they are about to be disappointed. No sooner have they arrived in town than they are being sought out by the local governor and stalked by the local sorcerer.

And it's here in Paphos that Saul chooses to become Paul. Being a Roman citizen, he would always have had two names, but it's here that he leaves behind the proud, kingly, Hebrew name of Saul and takes on the rather ordinary Roman name Paul, which means 'little'. Perhaps he does it because he knows he's called to the Gentiles; perhaps he does it because he wants to distance himself from his zealous, violent past. But perhaps he also does it because he wants to stay the right size. The visit to Paphos is a roaring success: the governor comes to faith and the sorcerer is stopped in his tracks – but Paul knows that he must never again get puffed up with pride and human success. His reputation and his message may get bigger and bigger, but he'll always need to be the 'little one' in the arms of his loving heavenly Father.

Father God, as I look ahead, I see so much that will stretch and challenge me, but I don't want to do it in my own strength. Help me to stay little – trusting your bigness to carry me through.

LYNDALL BYWATER

Little Paul, big God

But when the apostles Barnabas and Paul heard of this, they tore their clothes and rushed out into the crowd, shouting: 'Friends, why are you doing this? We too are only human, like you. We are bringing you good news, telling you to turn from these worthless things to the living God.' (NIV)

It seems there are numerous 40-something blind women with brown hair and black guide dogs walking the streets of the nation, and I keep getting mistaken for one or other of them. I wouldn't mind, but they all seem to have done impressive things! I'm forever being asked if I'm the woman who 'sang at our church recently', or who 'did that amazing sky-dive for charity', or who 'appeared on that TV quiz show the other week'. I'm a bit in awe of these women, so it's tempting to smile enigmatically and bask in their limelight for a moment, but you'll be pleased to know I never do.

Being mistaken for Greek gods is an impressive compliment indeed. Given that Paul and Barnabas had just narrowly escaped a stoning in Iconium, I often wonder if they were tempted to enjoy the misidentification for a while. Imagine a whole city believing you had supernatural powers and honouring you with the finest of gifts. Fortunately, these two young men, known as 'little' and 'son of comfort', weren't in the least interested in being worshipped. They knew the one who holds all the power and deserves all the glory.

Paul's journeys took him into all kinds of challenging situations. He needed courage, confidence, boldness and determination in huge quantities; but he didn't get them by bigging himself up. He found them, day after day, in the infinite love and greatness of his creator. He was content to remain little in the hands of a big God.

Are there things happening today that will require you to have more confidence and courage than you feel you have right now? If so, take heart from Paul. You may feel small and inadequate, but you are firmly held in the hands of a very big God.

Father God, strengthen me for today. Thank you that I don't have to have all the answers; thank you that I don't have to win the battles or prove my worth. Help me to let you fight for me.

LYNDALL BYWATER

From fences to bridges

'So now, not one thing separates us as Jews and gentiles, for when they believe he makes their hearts pure. So why on earth would you now *limit God's grace*?' (TPT)

I once heard an enthusiastic evangelist tell someone that the death of a famous politician's child was probably God's judgement upon him for the political decisions he had made. Perhaps the evangelist meant no offence, but I was appalled at the warped image of Christianity he painted. I only hope the man he was talking to hadn't ever lost a child of his own.

The gospel of Jesus Christ is good news for every single human being on this earth, and we get the privilege of sharing it wherever and whenever we can, but we also have a responsibility for how it comes across. We get to decide what flavour we give it, as we pass it on.

Acts 15 finds Paul and Barnabas in Jerusalem, meeting with the apostles to resolve some of the complex issues around Gentiles becoming followers of Jesus. Do they have to be circumcised? Which Jewish laws should they be obliged to observe? The Pharisees were clear – Gentile believers should do exactly the same things as faithful Jewish believers did. But most of the council disagreed. Interestingly, when the Pharisees talk about keeping the law of Moses (v. 5), the word 'keep' can also be translated 'put a fence around'. The apostles knew that Jesus had died to remove that fence once and for all, so that faith in him would never get bound up in religious rites and rituals. Only then could it be lived out in every culture on the face of the earth.

Paul himself had been a Pharisee, so it's a mark of his radical transformation that he was so willing to tear down those fences. From his conversion onwards, his message was seasoned with that extravagant grace which opens the way for anyone and everyone to come to Jesus.

Holy Spirit, as I talk about Jesus, may my words be grace-flavoured: not putting up fences that make people feel they're not good enough, but building bridges of kindness that help people walk straight into his arms.

LYNDALL BYWATER

Personality clashes

[Paul and Barnabas] had such a sharp disagreement that they parted company. Barnabas took Mark and sailed for Cyprus, but Paul chose Silas and left, commended by the believers to the grace of the Lord. (NIV)

Have you ever set out on a project only to have the plan completely rewritten halfway through? If you're the flexible, easy-going type, this kind of thing might not be a problem to you; in fact, you might positively welcome it. But if you're the idealistic type who likes things to go according to plan, having that plan completely rearranged can be frustrating.

Paul and Barnabas seem to have encountered something of a rearrangement of their plans shortly after leaving Jerusalem. What's more, it was the most painful kind of rearrangement because it involved conflict. Barnabas wanted to take John-Mark with them on their next mission trip, but Paul didn't. It's impossible to know what that disagreement looked like – whether they argued or whether anyone tried to mediate – but what we do know is that they eventually agreed to part ways. As we journey with Paul, you may begin to notice that he was a pragmatist. He understood that sometimes the best way to move forward was to let go.

Are you involved in something which has hit the buffers because there are differences of opinion that just can't be reconciled at the moment? It feels like a place of failure, doesn't it? Every instinct within us wants to find a way through. While the Bible puts a strong emphasis on working towards unity and reconciliation, Paul and Barnabas' story is evidence of the fact that sometimes the best resolution is to set each other free to go separate ways.

One of the most encouraging things about this sudden and dramatic change of plans was that it led Paul to find Timothy, one of the most important young leaders in the early church. Sometimes crises really do turn into opportunities.

Is there a situation where you know it would be more loving to part ways? If so, make a clean break: forgive any hurt the person may have caused you and pray blessing on them for the future.

LYNDALL BYWATER

People over projects

During the night Paul had a vision of a man of Macedonia standing and begging him, 'Come over to Macedonia and help us.' (NIV)

> God has entrusted us with his most precious treasure – people.
> John Ortberg

When he set out on his second missionary journey, Paul seemed to have a clear idea of where he needed to go. Perhaps he and the other apostles had devised a strategy for evangelising Asia Minor, before moving further afield. It would certainly have been logical to build on the work they had already done in the region. But God interrupted their plans by showing Paul a dream of a person crying for help. I wonder if it was meant to be a gentle reminder of that timeless truth that God always treasures people more than logical strategies. At that moment in time, there were people in Macedonia who needed him more than the whole region of Bithynia did.

So who were these treasures for which God was prepared to derail Paul's plans? Well, in the first instance, they were two women. Lydia was wealthy, whereas the slave was someone's possession. They could not have been more different in background or status, and according to the cultural norms of the day, Paul could reasonably have ignored them both – but he didn't. He taught Lydia the life-changing truth of Jesus' death and resurrection, and he demonstrated that same truth to the slave-girl by driving out the spirit which possessed her. This got him thrown into prison, but we don't hear him complaining about why God couldn't just have let him go to Bithynia like he'd planned. All we hear from the depths of that prison are songs of joy.

Paul knew that God treasures every single person he has ever made, and he counted it an honour to have his own plans derailed for the sake of finding and rescuing each precious person God sent him to.

Before you begin your plans for the day, why not stop a moment and ask God if he wants you to make time or space for a particular person? Is he entrusting one of his precious treasures to you today?

LYNDALL BYWATER

The art of listening

Then they took him and brought him to a meeting of the Areopagus, where they said to him, 'May we know what this new teaching is that you are presenting? You are bringing some strange ideas to our ears, and we would like to know what they mean.' (NIV)

I am part of a prayer community in Canterbury, and we have a little drop-in shop where people can come for a cuppa and a friendly chat. One of the things I most love doing, when I'm hosting there, is listening to people talk about what they believe. When we first opened, I used to feel a pressure to rush in and give people my explanation of the gospel, just in case I never saw them again, but we made a conscious decision that we wanted to focus on getting to know people, rather than preaching to them. And what I've learnt is this: when I listen to people, I also find myself listening to God and hearing what he wants me to say to them about himself.

Paul was used to turning up in a place, finding the local synagogue and teaching Jews and converts to Judaism about Jesus. But when he arrived in Athens, he had to find a different approach, because he needed to present his message to people who had no roots in his own religious tradition. So he went on a listening journey, walking the city, learning its ways and customs. He took time to listen to what the people there believed and, as he did, he suddenly heard the whisper of the Spirit telling him exactly how to introduce Jesus in that wholly pagan environment.

Where is God asking you to listen today? Is there a person whose story you need to hear? Is there a situation where you need to listen instead of talk? Sometimes we worry that, if we listen too much to the beliefs of others, we might get confused or pulled off track, so we close our ears; but it's often in hearing others that we most hear God.

Holy Spirit, thank you that every person I meet has a life that tells a story worth hearing. Give me grace and patience today to stop, listen and hear your whisper through the voices of those around me.

LYNDALL BYWATER

A place of oasis

One night the Lord spoke to Paul in a vision: 'Do not be afraid; keep on speaking, do not be silent. For I am with you, and no one is going to attack and harm you, because I have many people in this city.' (NIV)

During a particularly difficult season of my life, I remember God showing me a picture that gave me tremendous comfort. I saw myself on a bleak, muddy battlefield – a place which perfectly mirrored how my life felt at that moment. As I looked out over the scene, I noticed a spot of colour on the landscape. As I zoomed in on the spot in my imagination, what emerged was a red-and-white-striped marquee, a bit like the type you might get at a country fete. As I looked at it, I knew one thing for sure: there would be tea and scones inside. The thought made me smile, and I believe it was God's way of reassuring me that there would be moments of peace and comfort, even in the midst of my pain.

You've probably noticed by now that Paul ended up being opposed in almost every place he visited. Even for someone as determined as Paul, that must have been exhausting. Perhaps he expected Corinth to be the worst place yet, with its reputation for hedonism and lawlessness. But God provides comfort in the strangest of places, and despite the Jewish community being completely closed to him, that city turned out to be something of an oasis. He met lifelong friends there (Aquila and Priscilla), and he stayed for a year and a half, taking a break from the relentless travel and the almost relentless opposition.

Do you need a break from the battle? Even if that feels like an impossible dream, yours is the God who can do the impossible. If he wants to pitch a tea-tent in the middle of a war zone, he can. And he has not left you alone. He has people – his people – who can stand with you, love you and butter those scones.

Do you need to contact a close friend today, to tell them you're struggling and to ask for their support and prayers? Friends are a gift from God, and they can make all the difference in the hard times.

LYNDALL BYWATER

Works of power

God did extraordinary miracles through Paul, so that even handkerchiefs and aprons that had touched him were taken to those who were ill, and their illnesses were cured and the evil spirits left them. (NIV)

Remember that prayer drop-in shop I was telling you about? Well, there is another very important thing we do, in addition to listening to people's stories: we pray for them. Though we often get the opportunity to talk about Jesus, we find that people become far more curious about him – far more excited about the good news – when they start to see surprising and miraculous things happen in their lives.

Paul was an orator. His method of working was usually to arrive in a place and start debating with people, teaching them the truths of Jesus' life, death and resurrection. But he also knew that the Christian life was about more than mere words. The first people he met in Ephesus were keen, faithful Jews who had been baptised and were making a commendable effort at living life according to the teachings of John the Baptist and Jesus; but there was no power in their faith. It was honest and noble, but it lacked the Holy Spirit, and so it was incomplete.

Different church traditions have different understandings about how we receive the Holy Spirit as Christians. Some would say it's important to emulate the method Paul used here: the laying on of hands. Others would say God's Spirit will find and fill anyone who has submitted their life to Jesus and wants to receive him fully, regardless of the methodology. I suspect that Paul, the ultimate pragmatist, would say that it doesn't matter how it happens, but it does matter that you choose to welcome the power of the Holy Spirit to fill your life, so that he can work in and through you. It matters that you keep welcoming him afresh every day, so that he never gets boxed in, dampened down or shut out.

Holy Spirit, I welcome you again today. Soak those places in me which have gone dry; ignite in me a fresh fire of love for the people around me. Empower me to live a life of vibrant faith.

LYNDALL BYWATER

109

Opposing powers

Many of those who believed now came and openly confessed what they had done. A number who had practised sorcery brought their scrolls together and burned them publicly. (NIV)

Many years ago, I joined a team doing some evangelism in a small French town. We were going door to door, talking to people about Jesus. Most of the conversations were little more than brief brush offs, so we were particularly surprised when we met a lady who was thrilled to see us because she wanted help with some disturbing phenomena she was experiencing. Objects were being thrown around her home by an unseen force, and she occasionally found herself levitating from the bed. I think it is safe to say we felt a little out of our depth!

Paul had raised the stakes in Ephesus. Not only had he preached the kingdom of God with his words, but he had also demonstrated it by welcoming the Holy Spirit to do works of power; and now, other powers were feeling threatened. The lady we met in France knew that the supernatural phenomena she was experiencing were not the life-giving, hope-bringing miracles of a good God; they were the work of a malign presence in her home. Similarly, as the people of Ephesus saw the kingdom of God demonstrated in healing and blessing, many of them became aware that the supernatural powers at work in their city were of an altogether darker nature, and they wanted to be set free.

One of the most interesting aspects of today's story is what Paul didn't do. I have no doubt he and the church did a lot of praying, but otherwise he did very little. There is no record of him rebuking the exorcists who were operating in his name; he didn't speak to the crowds; he didn't stage a showdown with the goddess Artemis. He simply kept doing the task he'd been given, and he left it to God to silence those opposing powers.

Paul later wrote to the Ephesians about spiritual warfare, telling them to armour up and stand firm. Pray through Ephesians 6:10–18, choosing to put on that armour; then take your stand in the battle and trust in God.

LYNDALL BYWATER

The enemy within

'I know that after I leave, savage wolves will come in among you and will not spare the flock. Even from your own number men will arise and distort the truth in order to draw away disciples after them. So be on your guard!' (NIV)

> Two conflicting forces cannot exist in one human heart. When doubt reigns, faith cannot abide. Where hatred rules, love is crowded out. Where selfishness rules, there love cannot dwell. When worry is present, trust cannot crowd its way in.
> Billy Graham, *Hope for Each Day* (HarperCollins, 2017)

We've reached a sober moment in Paul's story. He believed he was on his way to death, so he set up a final coaching session. He had spent three years in Ephesus, one of the longest stays anywhere on his missionary journeys and they had all lived through some pretty tough times together. Given the sheer weight of enemy opposition they'd endured, you could be forgiven for thinking Paul would use this farewell speech to deliver some more teaching on how to handle attacks from pagan cults. But what he actually warns them of is something even more dangerous than anything Satan might have in mind: he warns them about themselves.

Attacks from an external enemy are real and possible, and we should be on our guard, but in truth it's the stuff inside ourselves which is always more likely to derail us. Billy Graham puts it brilliantly: if things like hatred, doubt, selfishness and worry start to shape us from the inside, it will be all but impossible to trust God and love others, and we'll run the risk of becoming arrogant and self-centred. Paul could see a time when proud, manipulative leadership would endanger that young church, and he wanted its elders to be alert and self-aware.

We all have moments of worry and selfishness; that's normal. The important question is whether we allow those things to shape us and our interactions with others.

It's a good habit to stop every so often and check what is shaping you. If you sense that fear and self-centredness are running the show, take a moment to ask forgiveness, and choose love and trust again.

LYNDALL BYWATER

Knowing you've heard

But Paul wouldn't budge… 'Why do you insist on making a scene
and making it even harder for me? You're looking at this backward.
The issue in Jerusalem is not what they do to me, whether arrest or
murder, but what the Master Jesus does through my obedience.' (MSG)

How do you recognise God's voice? That was the question I was asking
myself a couple of years ago. A thought had come into my mind, completely out of the blue, and it seemed to be a warning of something that
would happen to me. I wondered at length whether it was from God,
from my ever-churning brain or even from that malign force that seeks to
frighten and accuse. In the end, the answer lay in the feeling that accompanied the thought. Although the thought spoke of something potentially
difficult, there was no fear or confusion around it, just deep peace.

   The thought had entered Paul's head that it was time to go to Jerusalem. He seems to have been pretty certain from the outset that it was
a God-thought, but the people around him were keen to help him test
it. They discussed the logic and the wisdom of it with him – whether it
really made sense to go now, in the current political and religious climate.
They prayed with him, asking the Holy Spirit to confirm the right course
of action, and when Agabus brought his alarming word about Paul being
bound hand and foot, they probably assumed that was the clinching
proof that he definitely shouldn't be going anywhere near Jerusalem.

   But Paul recognised the feelings that accompanied the thought. Of
course he'd have felt nervous about returning to the Jewish Christian
community there; of course he'd have felt trepidation at knowing he'd
face imprisonment; but beneath it all was the deep peace and certainty
that only a true word from God can bring, and that was stronger than any
other feelings.

   How do you know when God has spoken? You know because he gives
you the peace and strength to act on his word.

---

*Lord, teach me to recognise your voice and hear the words you're speaking
to me. As I weigh up my circumstances and the opinions of others, help me
to hear the deeper resonances of your peace and your empowering.*

LYNDALL BYWATER

Making use of the past

The commander agreed, so Paul stood on the stairs and motioned to the people to be quiet. Soon a deep silence enveloped the crowd, and he addressed them in their own language, Aramaic. (NLT)

When I was a teenager, the story of Nicky Cruz had a profound impact on me. I remember watching the film *The Cross and the Switchblade* over and over again, marvelling at how someone so mired in crime and violence could be so completely transformed by discovering the love of God. Much of Nicky's life, since that remarkable conversion, has been spent reaching out to young people who are stuck in that same kind of gang culture, and I imagine they listened to his words with particular attentiveness because he knew exactly what it was like to be where they were.

That's the strategy Paul used when everything got very violent in Jerusalem. His own people were up in arms against him; even the Christian Jews hated him because they believed he was twisting God's law out of shape. By rights, he should have entrusted himself to the law enforcement officers who were trying to keep him from mob execution, but he had a more courageous plan in mind. These were his people; some of them were probably even his relatives. So he spoke to them in their native language, reminding them that he was one of them and that, not so long ago, he'd have been protesting in that crowd right along with them. And then he told them his conversion story. It didn't change their mood, but perhaps it reached a few hearts in that vast crowd; perhaps a few were able to discover the love of God because this man, who had been where they were, told them his story.

Your story is powerful. For people who are living the same sort of life you've lived, your story may be the very thing they need to hear, to help them discover the love of God for themselves.

What are the experiences which have shaped you? What difference has God made to you? What is your story? Could you tell it to someone today, either in person, or perhaps by writing it out and sharing it on social media?

LYNDALL BYWATER

Taking authority

'Now I urge you to take some food. You need it to survive. Not one of you will lose a single hair from his head.' After he said this, he took some bread and gave thanks to God in front of them all. Then he broke it and began to eat. (NIV)

Some years ago, I attended a meeting in the House of Lords. I'd visited the Palace of Westminster as a tourist before, but the experience of being there on official business was entirely different. Guided by the peer who was hosting us, we were waved through every locked door. You really do know when you're in the slipstream of someone with authority.

The last few chapters of the book of Acts are a lesson in authority. Something had happened to Paul during that turbulent time in Jerusalem, and he suddenly knew exactly where he was going. God had told him he would preach in Rome (Acts 23:11), and that knowledge seems to have given him a new courage to take authority over his circumstances.

When those circumstances included being aboard a ship in a storm, Paul could reasonably have been forgiven for doubting God, questioning what he had thought were certainties, and even fearing death – but he did none of those things. He knew he was on God's business, and he was hearing his master's word with uncommon clarity (vv. 23–25). It was Paul who reassured them, Paul who made sure they didn't starve and Paul who got every single one of those people safely to land again. When you are an ambassador for God's kingdom, you have an authority that can change situations and even save lives.

How often do you stop to remember that you have authority? You belong to the family of God and you have been appointed to help bring in his kingdom. When circumstances make others feel fearful or confused, you can use that authority to bring peace and courage into the room. Wherever you go, you carry the very Spirit of God, who is ready to work through you the moment you ask him to.

Be alert to situations where fear, confusion, negativity or stress seem to be running the show. Remember, you have authority to bring in the kingdom, so ask the Holy Spirit to change the atmosphere.

LYNDALL BYWATER

The right destination

For two whole years Paul stayed there in his own rented house and welcomed all who came to see him. He proclaimed the kingdom of God and taught about the Lord Jesus Christ – with all boldness and without hindrance! (NIV)

Adoniram Judson spent 40 years in Burma, suffering persecution, planting churches and translating the Bible. Dr David Livingstone went to Africa to find ways of ending the slave trade. Amy Carmichael was ill with neuralgia, but she knew she was called to be a missionary in India, so she travelled there, staying 55 years, rescuing orphans and liberating children from child prostitution.

For as long as the church has existed, people have chosen to put themselves in dark and difficult places, so that others might be saved and set free… and the apostle Paul was their trailblazer.

You may have noticed that we missed out a few chapters of Paul's story, so let me summarise them here. After his speech to the Jews of Jerusalem, Paul heard God telling him he would preach in Rome, and the next few chapters of Acts are the story of how that came about (Acts 22—26). At several points along the way, he could have opted out and gone back to his friends. The Romans weren't really interested in prosecuting him, so he could have laid low and carried on overseeing the many church plants he'd started. But Paul knew Rome was his destination, and he was determined. That meant continuing to contest his unjust treatment, and ultimately claiming his right to trial by Caesar. Given the political climate of the day, it was a suicidal mission, but Paul knew it was his mission.

Paul did eventually die at the hands of the Romans. Meanwhile, he got to teach and preach Jesus in the capital city of the Roman empire. Who knows how many thousands across Europe and the Middle East heard the gospel because Paul was obedient with the mission God gave him.

What's your mission? Perhaps it's not travelling halfway round the world or getting yourself arrested so you can preach to an emperor, but God has a purpose for your life, and he'd love to talk to you about it.

LYNDALL BYWATER

Seven parables of the kingdom

Caroline Fletcher writes:

The parables of Matthew 13 describe activities that occupied people in Jesus' day: sowing seed for crops, fishing with nets, baking bread by hand, even burying money in the ground to keep it safe. We may wonder whether parables so rooted in Jesus' time have anything to say about the issues we face today, especially when Christ introduced many of these parables with 'The kingdom of heaven is like…', a phrase that would have meant a lot to those listening to him then but little to most people now.

However, it is that mysterious phrase that can help us understand how these parables remain relevant to us. When talking of the 'kingdom', Jesus was describing not a place but God's activity as ruler: his kingship. The theologian John Drane helpfully explains the kingdom as 'God's way of doing things' (*Introducing the New Testament*, Lion, 1999). In his ministry on earth, Jesus taught that the kingdom of heaven had 'come near' (Matthew 4:17, NIV). In other words, through Christ's work, 'God's way of doing things' started to make a real difference in the world. However, he also taught that God's rule was not yet complete. People still resist God and, although at some point in the future everything and everyone will submit to him, for now there is an ongoing tension between good and evil with difficult consequences for us all.

Many of these parables deal with this tension and this is why they remain so pertinent today. Most of us will at some time have had our faith shaken by difficult things we have gone through. Most of us have been puzzled and disturbed, at times, to see Christians behaving in ways that seem out of keeping with their faith. Many of us will have wondered how the church can ever grow when the world seems so unreceptive to the gospel. These are all issues dealt with by these parables, so it has been really encouraging to look at them afresh and realise that they still have so much to say and so much hope and encouragement to offer us in a world which has not, as yet, submitted to God's rule.

Deeply rooted?

'But when the sun came up, the plants were scorched, and they withered because they had no root.' (NIV)

When I first became a Christian, I naively assumed that God would make my life easier. Imagine my shock when troubles occurred soon after finding faith! If I am honest, I still find myself knocked when difficult things happen. I need to pay closer attention to passages like today's. In our first parable, the parable of the sower, Jesus makes it clear that Christians will not get a smooth ride. The seed that falls on the rocky ground reminds us that 'trouble and persecution' come 'because of the word'. Christians do suffer and some fall away as a result.

Yet we do not have to respond to suffering in that way. The parable teaches that having strong roots makes all the difference. The rocky places had shallow soil which left no space for the plants' roots to fully develop. This left them unable to cope with the scorching sun.

How can we ensure we have strong roots to withstand trouble? In his book *When Answers Aren't Enough* (Zondervan, 2008), Matt Rogers converses with a couple who lost six children in a gas explosion. It was their close walk with God in the years before this tragedy that helped them cope. Their faith remained strong, for they had a deep, unshakeable knowledge of God's love to draw on. That is a challenge to us all, for it takes real effort to make time for God. As this parable teaches, we can so easily get distracted by the 'worries of this life' and 'the deceitfulness of wealth'. It is so easy for God to get squeezed out, for prayer to fade and for us to drift away from church. But we need to be prepared. The Christian life is tough; we need roots deep in God to stand firm in this fallen world.

How strong are your roots? Pray that God will show you if there are things he wants you to do to make your roots go stronger and deeper.

CAROLINE FLETCHER

Perfect timing

'But while everyone was sleeping, his enemy came and sowed weeds among the wheat, and went away.' (NIV)

In today's parable, a farmer's crop is spoilt by his enemy, who sows bad seed among the good. We can all relate to that picture. We live in a world where people mess things up. The question behind the parable is why God tolerates wrongdoing.

Before addressing that question, Jesus makes it clear that we should not blame God for the state of the world. The parable says that the farmer only sowed good seed; it was 'an enemy' that spoilt the crop, an enemy Jesus identifies as the devil. The world is not how God intended, just as the field was not as the farmer intended.

So God is not the source of evil, but why doesn't he stop it? Is God too weak or does he not care? This parable shoots those explanations down. It explains that one day God will eradicate evil completely but holds back from doing so not because he doesn't care, but because he cares so much.

In the parable, the weed that grows up is darnel. Initially, it looks just like wheat and the two can only be told apart when they have matured. However, by that time their roots are so entangled that the darnel cannot be dug up without damaging the wheat. They can only be safely separated at the harvest. Jesus seems to be saying that God has a right time to deal with evil. 2 Peter 3:8–9 suggests he delays tackling wrongdoing now in order to give people more time to turn to him. We can't fully understand this, for God's plans are beyond us, but it is reassuring. God can be trusted despite the state of the world: he knows what he's doing and, at the best time, he will put everything right.

Lord Jesus, help my faith to stay strong when I am struggling with the terrible things that go on in the world and when others hurt me. Help me to keep on trusting in your goodness and wisdom.

CAROLINE FLETCHER

From small beginnings

'Though it is the smallest of all seeds, yet when it grows, it is the largest of garden plants and becomes a tree.' (NIV)

We often hear reports that the number of Christians is declining. It's easy to feel disheartened at such news. The disciples must have felt like this at times too. Their Jewish heritage had taught them to expect a messiah who would instantly and dramatically change the world. However, Jesus was going about things less conspicuously and, while there were crowds following him, there were many, such as the religious leaders, who fiercely opposed him.

Jesus encouraged the disciples with his image of the mustard seed. From tiny beginnings, this little seed develops into an immense bush, big enough for birds to roost in. As I write this, I have lots of seeds growing on my windowsill. Some appear to do absolutely nothing for ages and when they do finally produce shoots, these often look puny and frail. It's difficult to imagine they will ever amount to anything. However, I have learnt that there is often no relationship between how they first look and what they eventually become – sometimes the tiniest seedlings go on to become the biggest and most beautiful plants.

The parable of the mustard seed is a great encouragement to us when it seems little progress is being made: when mission activities seem to bear little fruit or when we feel disheartened by our own spiritual progress. It reminds us that we are not struggling on alone; God is working quietly alongside us, bringing growth that may not, at first, be obvious or that might seem incredibly slow, yet will eventually go on to produce much more than we imagined. The disciples witnessed this principle in their own lives. This small, unpromising band of people, who so often let Jesus down, would go on to influence the whole world. Be encouraged; God is at work in you too.

Do you feel discouraged about your spiritual progress or the effectiveness of the activities you are involved in? Bring those feelings to God and ask him to help you see how he is at work in those things.

CAROLINE FLETCHER

We are not alone

'The kingdom of heaven is like yeast that a woman took and mixed into about thirty kilograms of flour until it worked all through the dough.' (NIV)

Have you ever made bread or pizza dough? It's always incredible to see how only a little bit of yeast can transform a much larger amount of flour. Jesus really stressed this point in today's parable by describing a woman making bread with a vast quantity of flour. The NIV says it was around 30 kilograms of flour! That would produce enough bread to feed more than a hundred people, all with only a small quantity of yeast.

Imagine, though, that you did not know about the power of yeast. It would be hard to believe a small amount of this unimpressive-looking material could do anything much. Sometimes we look at ourselves in a similar way. We can struggle to believe God can use us. Perhaps we hold back from helping in church or the community because we worry that what we have to offer is too insignificant. Maybe we suspect God wants us to get involved in something or start something new, but it just seems too overwhelming, rather like that vast quantity of flour, and we worry we just don't have what it takes.

Of course, the reality is that none of us does! However, as with the yeast, there is something more going on than we might assume. Just as there are forces mysteriously working away in the unimpressive-looking yeast, enabling it to transform vast quantities of flour, so we have God's Spirit empowering us. The yeast, though, doesn't have any impact if it stays in the packet: it needs to be mixed up with the flour. Similarly, we need to be where God wants us to be and doing the things God wants us to do if we are really going to see all God can do in and through us.

Do you tend to focus on what you can't do rather than what God can do through you? Ask God to show you how he wants to work through you to bring transformation to your workplace, community, home or church.

CAROLINE FLETCHER

The right motives

'The kingdom of heaven is like treasure hidden in a field. When a man found it, he hid it again, and then in his joy went and sold all he had and bought that field.' (NIV)

I became a Christian as a teenager and took my commitment very seriously. I made sacrifices, such as selling much of my precious record collection for charity, because I mistakenly believed it would impress God and persuade him to like me more. There was a lot of sacrifice, duty and guilt in my faith, but little understanding of God's love and acceptance.

Today's parable does teach about sacrifice but it also shows us what should be the motivation behind the sacrifice. In Jesus' day, it was commonplace to bury money to keep it safe. When the man in the parable discovered the treasure in the field, he 'sold all he had' to gain that treasure.

The parable teaches us that we will have to make sacrifices as Christians, for following Christ has to come before everything else. However, it also spells out that what motivated the man to sell everything was 'joy'. Putting God first should not be a grudging, miserable, guilt-ridden thing, but a joyful response to all he has done for us: his unconditional love and forgiveness. There is a cost to being a Christian, but as what is gained is so much more than what is lost, paying that price should be a no-brainer!

Do we follow Christ out of joy? Are we confident in God's love for us, or are we still trying to earn it? Sometimes past hurts can make it difficult to grasp how much God loves us. The book *Healing for Damaged Emotions* by David Seamands (Chariot Victor, 1981) has helped many who struggle with this. It certainly helped me, as did praying with others and talking honestly with God about how I felt. The Holy Spirit is a great healer and teacher; with his help we can get our motivation right.

Dear Lord, help me to know your love more. Heal me where past hurts make it hard for me to really believe that you love me unconditionally. Help me to serve you out of joy.

CAROLINE FLETCHER

Seeking the kingdom

'Again, the kingdom of heaven is like a merchant seeking fine pearls.'
(NASB)

Like yesterday's parable about the hidden treasure, the parable of the
pearl teaches that the kingdom of heaven is so precious that it's worth giving up everything for. Pearls were valued more highly than gold in Jesus'
day and so a fine one would be hugely expensive. The difference between
this parable and yesterday's is that the merchant in this story was actively
seeking the pearl and didn't simply stumble upon it by accident.

Today's parable fits well with Jesus' words 'seek first the kingdom of
God' (Matthew 6:33, ESV). As we saw in the introduction to this week's
notes, the kingdom is where God rules, where people are doing his will.
We do not stop seeking the kingdom when we become Christians, but we
continue seeking it as we go on walking with God and discovering what
he wants us to do with our lives.

It's easy, though, to forget to seek God's will over the day-to-day decisions we face, such as what job God wants us to do, what activities in
church we are called to be part of and where we should live. We can so
easily end up following certain paths just because they seem reasonable
or because we are influenced by what others think or by what everyone
else is doing. However, if our choices have not been directed by prayer,
we miss out. The pearl merchant would have seen many beautiful pearls
in his life, but he did not settle for the 'quite good' ones; he kept looking
for the very best. Similarly, there are lots of good things we could be doing
with our time and interesting paths we could go down, but God's way is
the very best for us and for those whom God wants to reach through us.

---

*Are there decisions you need to make or areas of your life about which you
have never sought God's will? Bring those things to God and ask him to
guide you and give you the strength to follow his will.*

CAROLINE FLETCHER

Casting the net wide

'Once again, the kingdom of heaven is like a net that was let down into the lake and caught all kinds of fish.' (NIV)

It can really rock our faith when we encounter difficult people in church. Shouldn't churches only contain loving and kind believers?

Today's parable helps us know how to view this issue. It describes an indiscriminate form of fishing in which a wide, weighted net was let horizontally down into the water. This net caught not only fish that were good to eat but other fish and creatures that were inedible. These were only separated from the wanted catch when the net was brought to shore. Jesus likened this form of fishing to evangelism: the net needs to be cast wide to reach as many people as possible, but this results in churches containing a mixed bunch of people who have chosen to belong for a wide variety of reasons. Just as there is a right time to bring the net in and separate the catch, so there is a right time for judgement – but it is not yet.

So where does that leave us now? It means we should have realistic expectations and not be surprised or allow our faith to be shaken by an imperfect church. You only need to read Paul's epistles to see that there were tricky people and troublemakers even in his churches, so there have always been such problems. Today's parable encourages us not to see this as a sign that Christianity is untrue or to take it as evidence that faith cannot change people. Rather than allowing our faith to be challenged by troublesome church members, let's pray for them to come closer to God. Let's also pray for ourselves to have God's strength to love them and his wisdom to know when to challenge their behaviour and when to bear with it.

Are there any people you find difficult in church? Spend time praying for those people and asking God for the grace, strength and wisdom to deal with them well.

CAROLINE FLETCHER

Divine makeovers

Jennifer Rees Larcombe writes:

God must have felt so frustrated! He is love, so he longed to lavish that love on the people he created – and to have their love in return. Yet most people found it impossible to relate to an invisible spirit they simply could not understand. That is one of the reasons why God came to us in the person of Jesus, so we could see his compassion in the eyes of a human, feel his gentleness in the touch of human hands and experience his love through a human smile.

Sadly, the close loving friendship that God enjoyed with Adam and Eve had been broken by sin. Because he longs for that level of intimacy with each of us, Jesus died to make it possible for that relationship to be restored. He took the punishment we deserved. Not only did he buy our entry to heaven, but he also made intimacy with God possible here on earth.

God also longs to restore us back to the people he designed us to be. When Jesus preached his first sermon (Luke 4:16–21) in the town where he grew up, he was burning to explain this, so he chose to read Isaiah 61. Everyone knew that the 700-year-old prophecy described the Messiah God had promised to send them, and Jesus added, 'Today this scripture is fulfilled' (Luke 4:21, NIV). He told them he had come to mend hearts broken by life's tragedies and the selfishness of other people – and to free others who had got themselves trapped in all kinds of darkness and misery. He explained that he wanted to remove the ashes of our broken dreams and plans, and exchange them for beautiful new things. He even promised to cover shame and loss with his supernatural joy, and to trans-form our pitiful little acorn-selves into massive oak trees. I do hope you'll have time to read the whole of Isaiah 61.

His hearers that day were so affronted that they tried to kill him but, ever since, he has quietly been doing all that Isaiah prophesised on a one-to-one basis – and he most definitely has done it for me! Over the next two weeks, let's look at some of the different ways God manages his 'divine makeovers' in the lives of ordinary people.

Sudden transformation

'Saul, Saul, why are you out to get me?' He said, 'Who are you, Master?' 'I am Jesus, the One you're hunting down. I want you to get up and enter the city… You'll be told what to do next.' (MSG)

God never does exactly the same thing twice, because he treats every one of us as uniquely individual. Some people are restored suddenly, but for others he takes a lifetime. Probably no one ever had quite such a rapid, lasting or dramatic restoration as the apostle Paul!

The Pharisees often appear as the villains in the gospel stories but Saul (or Paul as he became known) was the worst of the worst. Hell-bent on destroying everyone who followed Jesus, he was willing to kill or drag men and women off to prison. He was on a mission to purge Damascus of Christians when he met Jesus. Nothing was ever the same again!

He later described all his previous ambitions and judgemental rule-keeping as mere 'dog dung' and 'trash' in comparison to knowing and serving Christ (Philippians 3:8). His restoration not only meant giving up his previous lifestyle; it also changed him from what could have been described as a miserable, critical monster into one of the most joyful, positive people who ever lived. He wrote his letter to the Philippians from prison under a death sentence, but it bubbles with joy from start to finish.

That massive change happened for Paul instantly. Was your first meeting with Jesus like that or did your relationship form gradually over time? Sometimes, I meet people who feel worried because they cannot remember exactly when they opened their hearts to the Lord. I always assure them that it does not matter, so long as they know their hearts are open to him now. For some of us, getting to know God is a slow, lengthy process, while others move forward in a series of surges, or keep sliding backwards and need many restorations. How has it been for you?

Lord, sometimes I feel my life is rather insignificant and ordinary. Thank you, Lord, that to you I am unique and completely distinct.

JENNIFER REES LARCOMBE

Refreshing

They were all together in one place. Suddenly a sound like the blowing of a violent wind came from heaven… They saw what seemed to be tongues of fire that separated and came to rest on each of them. All of them were filled with the Holy Spirit. (NIV)

Here's another apparently sudden change: twelve men hiding in terror for weeks suddenly dashed out to preach boldly to thousands. People listened in astonishment and 3,000 of them were baptised that day.

Only weeks before, Peter, the man who did most of the talking, had been so scared when a servant girl thought he knew Jesus that he denied it with oaths. Thomas was plagued by endless doubts, and only one of them dared to stay with Jesus by his cross. What a difference now! When they were hauled before the Sanhedrin to explain themselves, their judges wondered what had transformed these 'unschooled, ordinary men' so drastically (Acts 4:13). No amount of flogging, threats or imprisonment seemed to stop them. So finally, the authorities were forced to conclude that they had 'been with Jesus'.

Actually, it was not so much that they had been 'with' Jesus, but that Jesus had changed them; now they were 'in Jesus' and had Jesus 'in them'. For three years, they had been 'with him', watching him, listening to what he said, while all the time he was gently chipping away at their weaknesses. Yet even that was not enough to transform them so dramatically. They, like the rest of us, needed Jesus himself, by his Spirit, to take up residence within, giving them – and us – access to all his qualities of courage, strength, wisdom, love and power.

I think most of us need this radical infilling of the Holy Spirit several times throughout our lives. Many say, 'But following Christ isn't about exciting experiences – it's attending church regularly, reading the Bible and praying.' And that's quite right, of course. But sometimes we need our relationship restored by what Peter described in another sermon as 'times of refreshing… from the Lord' (Acts 3:19).

Lord Jesus, I'm running dry and need more of you. Please refill me with your Holy Spirit.

JENNIFER REES LARCOMBE

Slow transformation

But Moses said to God, 'Who am I that I should go to Pharaoh and bring the Israelites out of Egypt?' And God said, 'I will be with you.' (NIV)

When we are young, we feel we can change the world, but disillusionment can seep in as the years go by. Moses had grown up with a huge sense of destiny. His mother saved his life by launching his cradle into the river, where a princess rescued and adopted him. He was educated in the world's most sophisticated court, but his birth mother never let him forget his Jewish roots. As a result, he came to see himself as the great saviour of his people, but in his enthusiasm went about the job totally the wrong way, by doing it all in his own strength. His efforts resulted in 40 years as a refugee in a wilderness, doing the most despised of jobs – shepherding someone else's sheep.

Have you ever failed an exam, lost a job or messed up an important relationship? Failure tastes horrible, and at 80 poor Moses had lost his self-confidence and become a nervous old 'no-hoper' with a stutter. All he had left were memories of missed opportunities and wasted potential. So why did God choose him to do one of the most difficult jobs of all time? Simply because, during those 40 years of exile, God had been restoring him into a man to whom he could talk 'face to face, as one speaks to a friend' (Exodus 33:11).

During our 'wilderness' times of frustration, it is easy to become bitter and disappointed with God. Instead, Moses had clung to him and developed a remarkably deep dependence on him.

The thought of the job terrified Moses, but God met all his objections by promising to be with him. The only qualification Moses needed for that huge task was to know that he couldn't do it but that God could. Knowing that simple fact has frequently transformed me, too.

Lord, please help me to stop exhausting myself endlessly trying to work out my own solutions. Teach me, as you taught Moses, that all I need is you.
                                                    JENNIFER REES LARCOMBE

The 'Why?' mystery

Job was a man who lived in Uz. He was honest inside and out, a man of his word, who was totally devoted to God and hated evil with a passion. He had seven sons and three daughters. He was also very wealthy… the most influential man in all the East! (MSG)

God was so proud of Job that, when Satan strolled into his throne room, he exclaimed, 'Have you noticed my friend Job?… [He's] totally devoted to [me]' (v. 8). 'Not surprising,' sneered Satan, 'You've lavished him with everything a man could want! Take it all away and he'll curse you!'

Poor Job. He was transformed from a prosperous, well-respected family man into a penniless outcast. Why? How could God let that happen to such a good person? Is he cruel or merely powerless?

The book of Job never explains the mystery of suffering, yet it has helped thousands of us through our dark experiences. Our human minds simply cannot understand why God stands back and allows his closest friends to go through terrible disasters. Disasters happen to us all and, when they do, Satan wants to use them to crush us while God longs to use them to lavish on us more blessings than we could possibly discover in the good times.

In spite of months sitting in the rubbish dump, ill and in pain, with his wife turning against him and his best friends telling him it was all his own fault, Job doggedly clung to his belief in God's goodness. Yes, he asked endless questions for 40 chapters but finally God gave him an amazing revelation of his power and Job received a deeper and more glorious realisation of who God actually is: 'I had only heard about you before, but now I have seen you with my own eyes' (42:5, NLT).

Sometimes, I've found it almost impossible to believe anything good could come out of my worst experiences, but now, looking back, I would say that they deepened my relationship with God far more profoundly than the good times ever did.

How would you say you benefited from your bad times?

JENNIFER REES LARCOMBE

A major key to restoration

When I kept it all inside… all the juices of my life dried up. Then I let it all out; I said, 'I'll make a clean breast of my failures to God.' Suddenly the pressure was gone – my guilt dissolved, my sin disappeared. (MSG)

I always start the day reading a psalm: all my favourites were written by David, perhaps because he had such a beautiful relationship with the Lord. Yet it's hard to fathom how someone who lived that close to God could stoop to adultery with a close friend's wife, then lie and murder to avoid discovery. Even more unbelievable is that it took him months before he realised he'd done anything wrong! The Lord had to send a prophet to let David know how deeply hurt he was (2 Samuel 12:1–12).

When my friend Debbie first became a Christian, her life was so utterly transformed that she said she felt wrapped in a warm glow of happiness. Then one day she arrived at my door in tears. 'I've lost my glow!' she sobbed. Hastily, I made tea and encouraged her to ask God what caused the glow to evaporate. She replied instantly, 'I was so mean to my mum last Sunday.' After she had asked the Lord's forgiveness and also phoned her mum, the glow soon returned.

Of course, there are many reasons for losing our sense of God's presence – depression, illness, grief and many others – but he always tells us if the cause was sin, because repentance puts it right so quickly (2 Corinthians 7:10). When there seems no obvious reason for losing our 'glow', we have to remember that he promised we would always have his presence with us, but he never promised we would always feel his presence. We just have to trust his promise.

David encountered Bathsheba when he had become rich, comfortable and too lazy to go off to war with his army (2 Samuel 11). Success and ease had taken God's place in his heart. God was only able to restore their friendship because David repented so completely.

David describes his grief vividly in today's psalm and also in Psalm 51. Mountaintops feel wonderful but are often far more dangerous than the dark valleys below.

JENNIFER REES LARCOMBE

Knowing we're loved

Jesus became visibly upset, and then he told them why. 'One of you is going to betray me.' The disciples looked around at one another, wondering who on earth he was talking about. (MSG)

I have to confess that John used to irritate me. How dare he say he was 'the disciple whom Jesus loved?' (John 21:7, NIV). Surely Jesus doesn't have favourites? I've always identified better with Peter, the impulsive action-man, and dismissed John as passive, drooping about on Jesus' shoulder, too good to be true! Then I discovered John was not always like that. When Jesus first met him, he had such an unpredictable temper that Jesus nicknamed him and his brother 'Sons of Thunder' (Mark 3:17). He seems also to have been a bit of a control freak, and when people refused to do what he wanted he was ready to destroy them with fire from heaven (Luke 9:54)! Driven by personal ambition, he tried to manipulate Jesus into offering him and his brother glittering careers in his future kingdom (Mark 10:35–37).

So what caused such a radical change? Perhaps his attitude began to change on the day of the quarrel John had with the other disciples over who was the most important (Mark 9:33–37). Jesus told them that unless they had the simple trust and dependence of a child, they could be nothing in his kingdom. A child who knows he's completely loved trusts a good parent completely. The key to John's restoration was knowing he was loved. When we really know that – it changes everything.

Had Peter been sitting next to Jesus in today's story, and Jesus given him the identity of the betrayer, Peter would instantly have taken charge and Judas would never have escaped to betray Jesus to the authorities. Peter even had a sword he was ready to use (John 18:10). Instead, Jesus told John – who by now trusted him so completely that he simply sat still and let Jesus be in control of the whole situation.

Do you have a situation in your life that you need to hand over to Jesus and allow him to work out in his own way, in his own time?

JENNIFER REES LARCOMBE

Restored relationships

The Lord said to me, 'Go, show your love to your wife again, though she is loved by another man and is an adulteress. Love her as the Lord loves the Israelites, though they turn to other gods.' (NIV)

I found Hosea's story a big help after my husband left me for someone else. I was devastated and desperately hurt but I felt profoundly comforted when Hosea showed me that God understands from experience exactly how painful rejection feels.

Hosea was a well-known travelling preacher, so his disastrous marriage must have caused widespread gossip. He adored his beautiful wife, Gomer, but after a series of affairs she left him to become a high-class prostitute. Hosea pours out his feelings of rage in the first of today's passages, but then he realises that God loves his people just as passionately as he had loved his wife. He was, in fact, sharing the fellowship of God's sufferings (Philippians 3:10). His anger sounds ugly, but it is totally normal when we've been badly hurt by someone we love. Did you notice the striking difference between our two passages? God must have drastically changed Hosea's heart, but Hosea must also have been willing to let him.

When Gomer's youth and looks were gone, she was finally hauled, destitute, to the slave market. Yet God asked Hosea to forgive and restore her. Everyone would have expected him to stone her to death – he had a legal right to do so; instead, he paid a high price for her and took her home to love and cherish as his wife. The preacher could then tell the astonished crowds, 'God loves you like I love Gomer. He sees you as his wife; it breaks his heart when you forsake and betray him. If you repent and turn back to him, he'll treat you as I have welcomed Gomer.' What a powerful visual aid! However hard we try, we cannot always restore broken relationships, but God longs for us to imitate Hosea's willingness to forgive.

Lord, I don't want to forgive and I'm not sure I ever can. But please help me to be willing – and change my heart.

JENNIFER REES LARCOMBE

Keep looking up

A woman was there who had been crippled by a spirit for eighteen years. She was bent over and could not straighten up... [Jesus] said to her, 'Woman, you are set free from your infirmity.' (NIV)

How I feel for this woman as I, too, live with spinal arthritis and scoliosis. Jesus has healed me of other things, so I wait in hope! My condition is not as serious as hers, but she would have lived with constant pain and, because her spine was so bent, she would have seen nothing except the floor, the dirt and dust of the streets, scattered rubbish, and camel and donkey poo – but never the faces of people she loved. Even sitting or lying, she could not see the stars, trees or distant hills. What a depressing view of life! When Jesus healed her, she would have gained so much more than just her physical restoration.

Sometimes, we can be disabled by our attitude towards life, and it is our joy which needs restoring. We can easily get into a habit of always looking *down* at the negatives, but it definitely changes the way we feel when we keep looking *up* to see something good, funny or positive in every situation.

There are people who need a lot more help from the Lord before they can begin to do this. Perhaps they have experienced nothing but rejection and disappointment all their lives; many people over the years have heaped pain upon them which has been stuffed into an enormous bundle that they have to carry on their shoulders until their spirits are bowed down – just as this woman's body was bent. They only ever see the dirt of the street, never the sunrise. It is useless to tell them, 'Cheer up!'; they simply can't without help. But I've often seen Jesus lift away that load of pain and replace all their 'ashes' with the beauty of new hope (Isaiah 61:3).

Sometimes, this kind of transformation takes him a very long time, like the fig tree in today's passage, but Jesus is wonderfully patient, just like the gardener in the story.

JENNIFER REES LARCOMBE

An impossible case?

Everyone wanted to see what had happened. They came up to Jesus and saw the madman sitting there wearing decent clothes and making sense… The man went back and began to preach… about what Jesus had done for him. (MSG)

My husband and I loved restoring furniture. We would buy old junk and then get to work repairing, polishing or repainting it until the original beauty and usefulness re-emerged. God loves to do the same with people, not turning them into something different, but restoring the person he always intended them to be.

We're not told what caused this man's dreadful condition: dangerously violent, he broke his restraints and 'night and day he roamed through the graves and the hills, screaming out and slashing himself with sharp stones' (v. 5). What a terrible way to exist. But shortly after meeting Jesus, he was washed, shaved, dressed and enjoying a beach breakfast.

Had he experienced some terrible trauma in his childhood, an unbearable loss or illness? His emotional pain left him vulnerable and Satan took control of his life, filling him with torment. Jesus calmly set him free and healed all the underlying causes, instantly.

Naturally, the man wanted to stay with Jesus; perhaps Jesus was the first kind person he had ever met. First, however, it was vital that his confidence and self-worth were restored, having had no value in anyone's eyes for so long. He needed a valued role, so Jesus entrusted him with telling the whole district about his healing.

A man I know, Bob, was disabled after a car accident caused by his own carelessness. A neighbour brought him to my church, and he was shown so much love that he gave his life to the Lord. However, always being on the receiving end of care made him feel diminished. It was not until he was given the vital role of sitting by the front door welcoming people, giving out service sheets and chatting to newcomers that he began to blossom. We all need to feel we matter to others.

Are you feeling discouraged about continuing to pray for someone who feels impossible to help? Remember Jesus said, 'With God all things are possible' (Matthew 19:26, NIV).

JENNIFER REES LARCOMBE

The elusive secret

I'm glad in God, far happier than you would ever guess…. I've learned by now to be quite content whatever my circumstances. (MSG)

When Lucy was baptised, she told the church how wonderfully the Lord restored her life. A year later, she had discovered that God does not always wave a magic wand and make our problems disappear.

When we discover the glorious fact that we are God's beloved daughters, we often feel we should be entitled to preferential treatment, and can feel angry and disappointed with him when he fails to answer our prayers. Yet God's priority is often to transform the way we think and feel about our difficult circumstances rather than changing the circumstances themselves, so that he can show us we 'can do all this through him who gives [us] strength' (v. 13, NIV). Sometimes, that requires a bigger miracle!

The apostle Paul had lived a hugely active life, travelling the world, speaking to thousands and planting churches wherever he went. How could a man with that much energy possibly say he was content and happy when he was chained in a prison cell, often cold, hungry and lonely and, as far as we know, never released? It must have been even more frustrating for him since he could remember how, during his previous prison sentence, God had sent an earthquake to release him (Acts 16:26–28, 35).

How could he possibly say he was 'happy' and 'content'? I guess, throughout our lives, we have to adjust to changes in our circumstances several times over. When that means not being able to do many of the things we have enjoyed before, we badly need to discover Paul's secret.

Perhaps we base our happiness on our surroundings, friends, job satisfaction and freedom to do what we like? Yet Paul appears to find his happiness, security and reason for living in a close friendship with God. He is 'glad' – not in his lifestyle, but 'glad in God'.

To find that kind of contentment in the difficult situations in which we are trapped, we need to be able to trust completely in God's ability to know exactly what is the very best for us.

JENNIFER REES LARCOMBE

Transformed through faithfulness

When his brothers saw that their father loved [Joseph] more than any of them, they hated him and could not speak a kind word to him. Joseph had a dream, and when he told it to his brothers, they hated him all the more. (NIV)

Joseph, at 17, comes across as a particularly obnoxious teen. God spoke to him in two dreams where he saw his whole family bowing to him reverently. They were intended to reveal the huge destiny God had placed over his life, and they came true years later, but it might have been wiser if he had not shared them at the time.

Have you ever felt that you had a promise from God about your future? Have you clung to it in spite of years of disappointment? I've met a lot of people who always knew God wanted to use them powerfully one day, however unlikely that seemed – until one day when God transformed their lives completely. Many of them told me how hard they had struggled to keep faithfully clinging to the Lord, whether he ever used them or not.

Joseph endured years of slavery and imprisonment, which would have been terrible for someone with such a brilliant brain. He must often have wondered if God had forgotten him, but through it all he stayed faithful to his God and quietly got on with doing the best job he could – within his restrictions – in spite of the boredom and disappointment. Was this the reason why God was able to transform him into the second most powerful man in Egypt?

Perhaps there was another reason why God could use this man to save not only Joseph's whole family but also the nation they would become: Joseph had such a forgiving heart. Throughout his childhood, his big brothers were obviously horrible to him, robbing him of everything that mattered to him. During his long years in Egypt, he could well have felt bitter. Yet, when he could have taken his revenge, he totally forgave, honoured and enriched them (Genesis 45:1–15).

When we know we have been given gifts by the Lord, yet other Christians refuse to recognise them or give us any encouragement, could forgiving them be an important factor while we wait for our breakthrough?

JENNIFER REES LARCOMBE

A life transformed

[Jesus] went into the synagogue and was teaching, and a man was there whose right hand was shrivelled… Then [he] said to the man, 'Stretch out your hand.' He did so, and his hand was completely restored. (NIV)

After some of the remarkable stories of restoration we've just been exploring, merely regaining the use of a hand doesn't sound too spectacular. Yet I believe it would have changed this man's entire life. He might have been born with this disability, like my little grandson, but I think it's more likely that some injury had caused the damage. Nowadays, it would not have been such a tragedy; physiotherapy would have helped or at least retrained his left hand and disability payments would have made his life easier. In those days, however, if he had been a craftsman, he and his family would probably have faced homelessness and destitution. How terrible for him to watch his children suffer like that – particularly if the accident had been his fault. His self-esteem and confidence would have shrivelled as fast as his hand. What a moment it must have been when, after the healing, he received his first week's pay packet!

Is there an area of your life which has shrivelled up? Perhaps it's your creativity? Once you loved art, singing or sewing, but the busyness of life has killed that part of you. You feel the gifted person you used to be has been turned into an automaton. Perhaps health problems or endless adversity have atrophied your zest for life.

It could be that your love for someone close has faded or even died: a parent, a husband or a stroppy teenager? There's no way we can *make* ourselves love someone, but we can ask the Lord to give us *his* love for them. As we begin to see them through his eyes, gradually he may restore our own lost love.

Have you lost your joy or confidence? Ask the God of restoration to bring these back to life, just as he gave everything back to that man in the synagogue.

JENNIFER REES LARCOMBE

A missed opportunity

Jesus looked at him and loved him. 'One thing you lack,' he said. 'Go, sell everything you have and give to the poor… Then come, follow me.' (NIV)

Jesus seemed to restore almost everyone he met. But there were some notable exceptions, which remind us that we all have the power to refuse him. The young man in today's story had such a privileged life that he probably felt he didn't need to be restored. Yet he saw something in Jesus that fascinated him, so he came to him with a searching question. Like many today, he had no idea who Jesus actually was, calling him 'good' and 'teacher'. The first thing Jesus did was to correct him by saying, in so many words, 'Only God is good, so either I'm God or I am wickedly misleading people. You need to decide.'

What an amazing transformation this man could have had, if only he had seen the love in Jesus' eyes; he could have spent time living with Jesus, become an apostle, written parts of our Bible, become famous down the centuries and been honoured throughout eternity. Yet we never learn his name; he stands as a terrible warning that a few years of riches, status and comfort can feel more important to us than eternity in heaven with the Lord.

Has something in your life become so important that it's crowding out the relationship with God you used to enjoy: your beautiful home and garden, your high-profile job, the sport at which you excel or the hobby that absorbs most of your time and energy? It could be the success of your children or, most common of all, has the job you do for God become more important to you than his company? The God who radically transforms us also requires radical commitment and longs for our friendship more than our service. To know God is to allow him to be God in our lives.

What would you say are the biggest hindrances to allowing God to transform our lives? Some examples might be: pride, success, achievement or an addiction to self-pity and negative thinking.

JENNIFER REES LARCOMBE

The good, kind father

'Put a ring on his finger and sandals on his feet. Bring the fattened calf and kill it. Let's have a feast and celebrate. For this son of mine was dead and is alive again; he was lost and is found.' (NIV)

I've left this story to last because it illustrates better than any other how God feels when he restores us. That young man behaved atrociously and was abominably selfish. His father must have heard news of his wild behaviour, yet he never stopped watching the road eagerly for his return. Some people who wander a long way from God feel they have so hope-lessly messed up their lives that God wouldn't want them back even if they dared to return. To read this story is to discover that God never gives up on us and is always keenly ready to welcome us home.

I love the way the father does not allow his son to crawl home and plead for help at the back door, then make him wait for long anxious hours to know how he would be received. Rich and dignified gentlemen in those days never hitched up their robes and ran down the road in pub-lic. Yet the father could not wait for the hugging and the kissing to begin. There was no way he was going to let his boy work like a slave to earn forgiveness or to prove he had changed; instantly, he was restored to his position as beloved son of the house. This story displays the very essence of God's nature.

Perhaps you are waiting for a prodigal to come home: a child, god-child, close friend – or even a husband? A daughter and son of mine both wandered away so far and got into such a mess that their lives seemed finished. Yet God restored them both dramatically. I think it was very important, as I waited, to ask God's forgiveness for any ways I had dampened their faith or failed them, and then to pray faithfully till they returned.

Lord, please help me never to be like the elder brother, but always to share the joy of your heart when I see you transforming someone's life.

JENNIFER REES LARCOMBE

Day by Day with God is on Instagram!

Follow us for a daily quote from *Day by Day with God*,
to help you meet with God in the everyday.

 Follow us: @daybydaywithgod

Recommended reading

Prayer in the Making
Trying it, talking it, sustaining it
Lyndall Bywater
978 0 85746 801 7 £8.99
brfonline.org.uk

Books on prayer can so often make us feel challenged but guilty. Not this one! *Prayer in the Making* is a book for everyone wanting to pray more confidently. Because we are all different, we need to find the prayer life that fits with who God made us to be. Lyndall Bywater explores twelve different types of prayer, helping us to find the ones which best suit us and our lifestyles. She certainly challenges us, but leaves us ready to talk confidently with God.

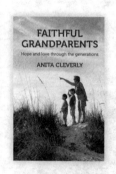

Faithful Grandparents
Hope and love through the generations
Anita Cleverly
978 0 85746 661 7 £9.99
brfonline.org.uk

Grandparents can be a vital link between a lived-out gospel and the faith of a younger generation. It takes courage and wisdom, humour and prayer, but the task of passing on the faith appears more significant now than ever before. A visionary book about the privileges and challenges of being a grandparent today; a book which brings soul food to the thriving as well as the hungry, weary and disappointed.

To order

Online: **brfonline.org.uk**
Telephone: +44 (0)1865 319700
Mon–Fri 9.15–17.30

Delivery times within the UK are normally 15 working days. Prices are correct at the time of going to press but may change without prior notice.

Title	Price	Qty	Total
Prayer in the Making	£8.99		
Faithful Grandparents	£9.99		
Day by Day with God (May–Aug 2019) – single copy	£4.60		
Day by Day with God (Sep–Dec 2019) – single copy	£4.60		

POSTAGE AND PACKING CHARGES			
Order value	UK	Europe	Rest of world
Under £7.00	£2.00	£5.00	£7.00
£7.00–£29.99	£3.00	£9.00	£15.00
£30.00 and over	FREE	£9.00 + 15% of order value	£15.00 + 20% of order value

Total value of books	
Postage and packing	
Total for this order	

Please complete in BLOCK CAPITALS

Title .... First name/initials .... Surname..

Address..

.... Postcode ....

Acc. No. .... Telephone ....

Email...

Method of payment

☐ Cheque (made payable to BRF)   ☐ MasterCard / Visa credit / Visa debit

Card no. ☐☐☐☐ ☐☐☐☐ ☐☐☐☐ ☐☐☐☐ ☐☐☐☐

Expires end ☐☐ M M ☐☐ Y Y   Security code* ☐☐☐   Last 3 digits on the reverse of the card

Signature* .... Date .... /............ /............

*ESSENTIAL IN ORDER TO PROCESS YOUR ORDER

Please return this form to:

BRF, 15 The Chambers, Vineyard, Abingdon OX14 3FE | **enquiries@brf.org.uk**
To read our terms and find out about cancelling your order, please visit **brfonline.org.uk/terms**.

The Bible Reading Fellowship (BRF) is a Registered Charity (233280)

Each issue of *Day by Day with God* is available from Christian bookshops everywhere. Copies may also be available through your church book agent or from the person who distributes Bible reading notes in your church.

Alternatively you may obtain *Day by Day with God* on subscription direct from the publishers. There are two kinds of subscription:

Individual subscriptions
covering 3 issues for 4 copies or less, payable in advance
(including postage & packing).

To order, please complete the details on page 144 and return with the appropriate payment to: BRF, 15 The Chambers, Vineyard, Abingdon OX14 3FE

You can also use the form on page 144 to order a gift subscription for a friend.

Group subscriptions
covering 3 issues for 5 copies or more, sent to one UK address (post free).

Please note that the annual billing period for group subscriptions runs from 1 May to 30 April.

To order, please complete the details on page 143 and return with the appropriate payment to: BRF, 15 The Chambers, Vineyard, Abingdon OX14 3FE

You will receive an invoice with the first issue of notes.

All our Bible reading notes can be ordered online by visiting
biblereadingnotes.org.uk/subscriptions
For information about our other Bible reading notes,
and apps for iPhone and iPod touch, visit
biblereadingnotes.org.uk

All subscription enquiries should be directed to:
BRF, 15 The Chambers, Vineyard, Abingdon OX14 3FE
+44 (0)1865 319700 | **enquiries@brf.org.uk**

DAY BY DAY WITH GOD GROUP SUBSCRIPTION FORM

All our Bible reading notes can be ordered online by visiting
biblereadingnotes.org.uk/subscriptions

The group subscription rate for *Day by Day with God* will be £13.80 per person until April 2020.

☐ I would like to take out a group subscription for .... (quantity) copies.

☐ Please start my order with the September 2019 / January 2020 / May 2020* issue. I would like to pay annually/receive an invoice* with each edition of the notes. (*delete as appropriate*)

Please do not send any money with your order. Send your order to BRF and we will send you an invoice. The group subscription year is from 1 May to 30 April. If you start subscribing in the middle of a subscription year we will invoice you for the remaining number of issues left in that year.

Name and address of the person organising the group subscription:

Title .... First name/initials .... Surname ....

Address...

.... Postcode ....

Telephone .... Email ....

Church..

Name of Minister ....

Name and address of the person paying the invoice if the invoice needs to be sent directly to them:

Title .... First name/initials .... Surname ....

Address...

.... Postcode ....

Telephone .... Email ....

Please return this form to:
BRF, 15 The Chambers, Vineyard, Abingdon OX14 3FE | enquiries@brf.org.uk

To read our terms and find out about cancelling your order, please visit **brfonline.org.uk/terms**.

DAY BY DAY WITH GOD INDIVIDUAL/GIFT SUBSCRIPTION FORM

To order online, please visit **biblereadingnotes.org.uk/subscriptions**

☐ I would like to give a gift subscription (please provide both names and addresses)
☐ I would like to take out a subscription myself (complete your name and address details only once)

Title .... First name/initials .... Surname ....

Address ....

.... Postcode ....

Telephone .... Email ....

Gift subscription name ....

Gift subscription address ....

.... Postcode ....

Gift subscription (20 words max. or include your own gift card):

....

....

Please send *Day by Day with God* beginning with the September 2019 /
January 2020 / May 2020 issue (*delete as appropriate*):

(*please tick box*)	UK	Europe	Rest of world
1-year subscription	☐ £17.40	☐ £25.50	☐ £29.40
2-year subscription	☐ £33.00	N/A	N/A

Total enclosed £ .... (cheques should be made payable to 'BRF')

Please charge my MasterCard / Visa credit / Visa debit with £ ....

Card no. ☐☐☐☐ ☐☐☐☐ ☐☐☐☐ ☐☐☐☐

Expires end ☐☐☐☐ Security code* ☐☐☐ Last 3 digits on the reverse of the card

Signature* .... Date ....../....../......
*ESSENTIAL IN ORDER TO PROCESS YOUR ORDER

Please return this form to:
BRF, 15 The Chambers, Vineyard, Abingdon OX14 3FE | **enquiries@brf.org.uk**

To read our terms and find out about cancelling your order,
please visit **brfonline.org.uk/terms**. The Bible Reading Fellowship is a Registered Charity (233280)

DBDWG0219